ADJUSTING FOR LEADERSHIP

DR. BEN DUKE

"Experience is the hardest kind of teacher. It gives you the test first and the lesson afterward."

-Oscar Wilde

INTRODUCTION

Dear Reader,

When I set out to write a book to help people navigate their way through life and the complex world of business, I naturally was compelled to share my story. I'm blessed to have reached a certain level of success, but the journey itself was full of many mistakes and hard lessons. Bottom line—it's my purpose in life to help people influence themselves to accomplish their goals and achieve their full potential.

Being a risk taker at heart, I didn't want to take a mundane approach with my first book, so you'll see a few departures from the normal literary confines of most books. Instead, I chose to take creative license. Forgive me. For instance, you'll notice this book is written in the first person, but is told through the eyes of Mr. Bill Samson. Bill and I have a lot in common; many of his stories mirror my own experiences.

I've also changed many of the names of the characters to protect their identities. And rest assured that no animals were harmed in the telling of this story...

Enjoy this tale. I hope this allegory will assist you in your endeavors!

My Very Best,

Dr. Ben Duke

PURPOSE

Dear Bianca,

As I watch you sleep, looking into your innocent face, my heart fills with gratitude. You are always with me, in my thoughts and in my heart, as I take each step to improve my life so that I can be a better example for you.

The fact is that you saved me, young lady, even before you could speak. But I'll save that story for another time.

Looking back, I have always been a driven person. In my heart, I knew I had to make something of my life. I grew up watching my mom, your nana, work multiple jobs day and night while raising two boys on her own. Early on, she shared a small twin bed with my baby brother, while I slept on a pull-out that filled the rest of the room.

I swore my life would be different and I promised to make a difference for others in this world. As I made my way through life, I discovered that every person creates their own blueprint. Each person must decide what they want to do, who they want to be and how they want to benefit the world.

It's my hope that you see the world as I do, abundantly there to support your vision and dreams. Life will not always be easy, but the journey is the greatest part. And remember, no matter what, I'm your biggest fan.

No matter which profession you choose, follow what you truly love to do and you will succeed beyond your wildest dreams. That is the truth to living a fulfilled life. When you follow that route, the world will open for you to explore. I chose to become a chiropractor, but the blueprint for success in business and life follows the same path.

The only limitation for your mind is your own imagination. So, dream to the heavens! Nothing and no one can stop you – but you. I'm here to guide and help you avoid the pitfalls of the average, the mundane people who adopt a mediocre mindset. You were made for more than that. Now, some people might try to tell you that you can't follow your dreams, because they didn't follow theirs. Don't listen! Lead your own life, and eventually others will follow.

Always pursue your purpose in life. It may take time. It may take years of searching, but that's OK. No matter how long it takes, follow that purpose with all your heart. It will cultivate your drive, willpower, courage and conviction. Through these virtues, you will serve the world well.

I will always be there for you.

Love,

Dad

ONE

I was doing my best to cram three days of clothing into my worn duffle bag, when a blue knit sweater came flying at me, smacking into my head. It smelled like the inside of my old locker room during summer practice.

"If you're going to take my clothes hostage and sweat all over them, try cleaning them after," I said balling it up and flinging it back in his direction. "It's good manners."

The sweater hit him squarely in the chest and he gave an exaggerated moan as he fell over backward onto his bed. "Not your fastball," he cried. He then propped himself up on his right arm. "Maybe you should have been a pitcher when you played."

I grinned and shook my head. "I enjoyed hitting too much."

He sniffed the sweater before putting it on. "It's good for another day."

I rolled my eyes at him, before I zipped up my bag. "I'll be back

Sunday night. Hey, since I'm *loaning* you my sweater, can I have the Chem notes from this morning?"

"Sure, Bill. I got you covered," he said. "That double major is kicking your butt."

I shrugged. "I like to work hard and play hard, you know that."

He shot me a crooked smile. "So, does that explain why you didn't make it to class this morning?"

I dropped my head and sighed. "I was a little hung over."

"Lucky for you, you have a roommate that can't afford to skip class," he said, handing me his notebook.

"Thanks, Bobby," I said. "I'll have it back to you before Monday. I promise."

I needed to get home before it got dark. A half dozen people waylaid my progress as I made my way to the car. I received various invitations to parties going on that weekend, but I'd have to miss them all. Mom's birthday party was more important.

I slung my bag into the backseat, hopped in the driver's seat, and turned the key. Nothing. *Not now*, I thought, leaning my head back. I knew the sedan needed a new ignition, but it was either that or text books. *Come on*, I silently encouraged her. *Just get me home.* Then I added, *And back again.* After a few more attempts, it started up and I breathed a sigh of relief.

I listened to Dave Matthews Band for the first half of my journey, then let the radio serenade me the rest of the way home. I wondered what mom would have in the crockpot for dinner. My stomach grumbled as I thought of her pot roast.

When I pulled into the driveway, I turned the motor off and sat for a moment. Sunset gave my childhood home a warm glow. It seemed so surreal, not matching my memories. *Home sweet home*, I thought. Even my self-talk was mocking at times.

The small two-bedroom house sorely needed a new coat of paint. One of these weekends I'd put the time in. Who else would do it? Certainly not the landlord.

As I stepped out of the car, Jacob raced quickly to the front door like the beagle we had growing up. "You're early!"

"Yeah, I don't have any classes Friday afternoon."

"Sweet! I wish it worked that way in high school."

I laughed. "Give me a break. You have it easy, bro."

"Says you."

As I walked in the front door, I couldn't help but shudder slightly. The thermostat was set to its normal, sixty-five degrees, but that didn't account for my sudden chill. No, that was probably due to the fact that it always felt like I was entering some sort of time warp whenever I came home.

Jacob ran to his room as I stood rooted, feeling like the floor was made of putty. I scanned the family pictures on the wall. One of me in my little league uniform caught my eye; I had a goofy grin with two teeth missing.

Also missing were any photos of my father. He was booted out when I was ten, never to return. Still, he'd left his mark. More on my mom than me, but still...

"What do you call that performance tonight, Billy Boy?" his words still echoed like a ghost in the walls.

"I dunno," I'd mumbled, looking to the floor.

"It was like you were blind as a bat out there. I was ashamed to be sitting there on the home team bleachers. What were you swinging at anyway? You looked like a fool in front of everyone."

I could only hang my head and wait for the barrage of insults to stop. "Sorry," I had offered weakly. To this day, I don't know why I always apologized to him.

Dad enjoyed squeezing my upper arm so hard it bruised. "Not much meat on you. Baseball's about all you're good for."

"Bill!" Mom's sweet, enthusiastic voice pierced through my reverie, bringing me back into the present. I grinned as she settled into my chest with a hug. "Why didn't you come into the kitchen? How long have you been standing here?"

"Not long," I said, holding her tightly, not willing to let her go quite yet. "Happy birthday, Mom."

TWO

After dinner, Mom looked like she was struggling to keep her eyes open. I guessed that she'd been up since four, so I playfully pushed her out of the kitchen when she tried to clean up.

"We'll take care of the dishes," I said.

She turned back to give me an appreciative look. "Thank you."

"We're going to what?" Jacob asked in a stage whisper.

I tried to shush him, but Mom just laughed. "Leave them. I'll do it in the morning."

I kissed her gently on the cheek. "I loved the pot roast, mom."

She limped up the stairs, like she was hiking through snow. Working three jobs was taking its toll on her aging body. I shook my head, watching her disappear around the corner, before I walked back into the kitchen.

"You weren't serious about the dishes, right?" Jacob whined.

I chuckled. "It's not that bad. I'll wash, you dry. Just like the good ol' days."

When everything was tidied, I went to the fridge and pulled out two cans of pop. No beers in Mom's house. "Come outside with me for a bit," I said. "We can catch up."

The porch light was out, but the full moon more than made up for it. I sat down on the cushioned chair and looked over a Jacob, who leaned against the rail.

"How did mid-terms go?" I asked.

He gave a gruff sound that made me laugh.

"That good, huh?" I asked. "What do you do all day, anyways?"

"I dunno."

"It gets harder in college, you know."

"Who says I'm going to college?"

I frowned. "Mom, for one. She'd be disappointed if you didn't get a degree."

"You're going. That's enough. I don't have to," he said with a shrug. "School isn't my thing. Besides I could never qualify for any kind of scholarship, not like you did."

"So, what's your plan? What will you do?"

"Make money," he said quickly.

"Yeah, but how?"

"What do you mean? I'm doing it now."

"Selling home security systems? That's your big plan?" I folded my arms across my chest and leaned back. "You can't make much that way."

"Yeah, I know," he said, sitting forward. "I can't tell you what I'll be selling when I graduate, but I can tell you that I'm going to make a lot of cash. I have plans. They just don't include college."

"So, you like selling."

"Yeah."

Giving an exaggerated shudder, I said, "I hate sales."

"It's not that bad."

I paused and gave him a deliberate grimace. "Yeah it is."

His lips twitched into a small smile. "What are you going to do when you graduate? You're in your third year."

"I'll do something in medicine. I want to make good money and really have the chance to help people."

Jacob shook his head, "That's way too much work. Way too much studying."

I waved my hand. "Oh, I enjoy that. It's a challenge."

"Do you still have your eye on that Mercedes? That black on black CLS 550 Mercedes?"

"You got that right!" I nodded, slipping into a comfortable fantasy. "Love that car, very sleek with performance wheels and leather seats. I've got it all picked out."

"It's a far cry from Mom's old clunker you drive now."

"At least I have wheels," I muttered. "Still taking the bus?"

"Whatever."

We were silent for a moment, each lost in our own thoughts. Finally, Jacob murmured something under his breath as he looked away.

"Hm?" I asked.

Jacob turned around and looked me in the eye. "You might not believe me, but I'm going to make it."

I stared at him for a moment, wondering where that come from. "I never said you wouldn't," I replied, furrowing my brows. It was so like Jacob to make such a big deal about nothing.

He jutted out his chin. "But you think that."

"What? You're a mind reader now?"

"Never mind," he said, turning away again. "It doesn't matter."

Looking at his profile, I could tell he was genuinely upset and that bothered me more than I wanted to admit. "Jacob, look at me," I said leaning forward with a sigh, waiting for him to turn his gaze back at me. "What's this all about?"

"I don't know."

"Yes, you do," I said with a dismissive wave of my hand. "Don't cop out."

He took a moment, then let out a ragged sigh. "You're always telling me that I'm not doing enough. That I'm not working hard enough."

"Yeah, so?"

"So, it's not true. I do work hard."

I wanted to laugh at him, tell him how he didn't know what work was, but then it hit me. That sort of biting comment wasn't exactly helping. He didn't want to hear that, not from me. I sat back and considered the soon-to-be-man in front of me. Yes, he was my little brother, but he was also seventeen. It wouldn't be long before he'd be stepping out on his own.

So, instead of barking out a few insults, engaging in a fresh battle, I swallowed my pride and nodded. "You're right."

"I am?" He looked so genuinely surprised that I couldn't help but laugh.

"Yeah. You are. You *do* work hard. I don't give you enough credit for that. There aren't that many kids out there working a job like you, while finishing up high school. And I can tell you're doing pretty well at it."

"I am," he said, straightening his shoulders up a bit. "The boss just gave me a fifty cent raise last week."

"Hey, that's great," I said, feeling a rush of pride for him. Suddenly, it hit me. How many times had my pseudo-praise for him come out as condescension? I sounded like Dad too often.

Jacob's eyes widened. "You really mean it?"

I nodded. "Yeah. I do."

He smiled and said, "I like the work. It's fun. And I think I really have a knack for selling. I mean, there are weeks I'm the top salesman. And you might not know it, but I'm the youngest one there!"

I smiled back, realizing he'd never shared anything like this with me before. It felt good. "I'm proud of you, little brother."

The look he gave me was priceless. His shoulders relaxed and his smile widened. It was amazing to me what a few words of praise could do. My little brother looked like he could conquer the world!

THREE

While I was home, I thought it would be smart to get a chiropractic adjustment from Dr. Simon Tracy. I hadn't made an appointment, but knew he would accept me as a walk-in, given our history.

"Bill, it's good to see you," his elderly receptionist beamed at me. "You back for Nancy's fiftieth?"

I nodded in awe. Helen always remembered me, but I was surprised she knew it was Mom's birthday. And even which one. "Now, how did you know that?"

She tapped the side of her head. "Steel trap, my boy. Memory's as good as it was when I was your age."

I grinned at her. "You think Doc can see me today?"

"Of course," she said. "You might have to wait a bit, but he'll see you as soon as he can."

"No hurry," I replied, turning to take a seat. I started walking around the room, looking at all the quotes on the walls. They always filled me with inspiration. One in particular made me feel energized every time I read it: "The main reason a person does not reach their desired goal is because their connection with the goal was not strong enough."

I smiled as my mind wandered back to the first time I'd stepped foot in the office. Mom had to help me through the front door, as I'd hobbled across the dark blue carpet. My lower back throbbed and it had taken all my concentration not to yell out in pain. Being that it was Sunday, the waiting room had been completely deserted. I shook my head in wonder that any doctor would actually be willing to come in on a *Sunday* to see me.

"What seems to be the trouble?" Dr. Simon's face creased with genuine concern crossing his face.

"It's my lower back," I said with a wince.

He nodded. "When did it start?"

"Two weeks ago."

"Any idea what caused it?"

I shrugged. "It was fine up until the time it wasn't. Must have tweaked something on the ball field. I just don't know what it was exactly."

"That's pretty common," he said, gently guiding me across the room toward his black leather exam table. I remember moving slowly, feeling like an old man. He was patient, moving at my pace, putting all his attention on me.

"What position do you play?" he asked.

"Third base."

He nodded. "Love the game. I was an outfielder in high school."

"My dream is to make the pros," I said as a sharp pain shot up my back. I couldn't stop the whimper from escaping my lips. "At least that *was* my plan. Looks like I'll need to find a new goal in life."

"So, what have you done for treatments so far?"

I looked at my mother and when she nodded, I shrugged. "Some drugs. They wanted me to get an MRI, but it was too expensive."

"We don't have insurance," my mother added, her eyes cast down. "I just couldn't afford it."

Dr. Simon nodded. "Those run a few thousand, I know. What drugs did they give him?"

"A heavy dose of Vicodin and a muscle relaxer."

His brow creased as he turned to me. "Is that helping much?"

"Not really, maybe for a little while, but I feel like it's just temporarily numbing the pain. I don't like taking them. They make my stomach upset and my head feel weird."

"Well that's not good. Let's see what we can do." Dr. Simon proceeded to ask me many questions. He did a thorough inspection and evaluation of my back. After about an hour, he sat down and said, "You have a disc bulge pressing against your spinal cord. The good news is I think we can help."

Over the next three weeks, Dr. Simon worked with me and I began to heal and recover. After having endured two weeks of agony with no hope for improvement, Dr. Simon's treatments had been nothing short of a miracle. He would always hold an important place in my personal Hall of Fame.

"There's my favorite college student," Dr. Simon's voice pulled me out of my daydream. "How have you been?"

I looked up at his welcoming face. His short brown hair was now peppered with a few more gray ones. Smiling, I said, "Great, Doc. Just thought I'd come in for a tune up."

"Good idea!" he said. "Come on in here."

As Dr. Simon adjusted me, he remained quiet. When he was done he gave me a light pat on my right shoulder and said, "OK, you can sit up now."

I got up slowly, tested out my newly adjusted body and smiled. "Feels good."

"I'm glad," he said warmly.

"Must be nice," I said.

"Hm?"

"You know. Helping people."

"It is," he said with a smile. "There's nothing like it, actually."

I nodded and paused for a moment before saying, "I still haven't figured out what direction to go. Something medical, but not sure what."

"Why medical?"

"Playing in the pros wasn't an option anymore."

I smiled. "No, I meant, why help people through medicine?"

"There are a few reasons," I said with a shrug. "Got the double major in biology and chemistry, so I can keep things open."

Dr. Simon looked at his watch and said, "You're my last patient of the day. To be honest, I worked straight through and completely forgot about lunch. I'm starved! Can I buy you dinner?"

As if on cue, my stomach growled. I laughed. "Sure, I can eat."

"When I was in college, I was always hungry."

We walked down the street a few blocks to a little mom and pop diner, ordered and sat down. After a few bites, Dr Gold put down his fork and said, "You have a big decision ahead of you. I wanted the opportunity to encourage you to choose chiropractic."

I nodded hesitantly, but remained silent. Although I'd considered becoming a chiropractor, I wasn't leaning in that direction. My eyes were on the big prize. I had always seen myself as a well-respected medical doctor, who could set his own hours and golf on the weekends while enjoying a beautiful suite in the city.

Dr. Simon read me like a book. Laughing, he said, "OK, why not?"

"I don't know. It just didn't seem like a good option."

"I think it would suit you." He paused, waiting for me to say something. When I didn't, he continued, "So, what's your vision? What do you want out of life?"

"Well, you know how much our family struggled. Right?"

He nodded. "I do."

"So, I definitely want to make money. Lots of it," was my immediate no-brainer response. "I plan to be able to buy anything I want. Also, I really want a family and give my kids anything *they* want."

I'd like to do better than Mom could growing up.

I immediately felt a pang of guilt course through me. Mom had done so much for me. She still did. My thoughts left me feeling like a disrespectful and ungrateful child. Still, I remember the nights that mom had to stretch the soup, feeding us crackers to fill the never-ending hunger in our stomachs. As a result, I had a burning hunger to succeed in life.

Dr. Simon nodded thoughtfully. "Sure, sure. Money's important. No doubt about it. It's just that..." he paused for a moment, then continued, "I think you'll find, it isn't what will make you happy in the end."

Thoughts of my Mercedes, fine dining, extravagant trips around the world all flitted through my mind. "I don't know. I think financial freedom would go a long way toward making me happy," I said, giving him a grin.

Dr. Simon laughed. "True. It's just that money as a motivation won't work, not really. It'll fade over time."

"Maybe."

"So, what is it that you really want to *do* in life? After all, making money isn't really a goal. It's a reward."

I sat back and thought about it. In the space of a few moments, I felt the tingling of excitement deep inside when I realized I knew the answer. I'd always known the answer. I looked at Dr. Simon and said, "I always wanted to help people."

"Ah, see, now there is a worthwhile goal!" he exclaimed so loudly that the people next to us looked over. Quieting his voice, he continued, "So, now, the challenge is to find something you can do that will help others, while still allowing you to make the money you desire."

I nodded. I'd always pictured myself in a gorgeous penthouse suite overlooking Manhattan, hosting non-stop parties on the weekends. How empty I'd feel if I wasn't helping others.

For some reason, I'd never pictured myself becoming a chiropractor. Sure, surgeons and medical doctors helped people all the time. They were important and had a purpose. However, the fact was that a chiropractor, the chiropractor in front of me, had made such an impact on my life five years ago. The idea that I could possibly help another in that way filled me with a powerful sense of joy. That option was suddenly overwhelmingly appealing.

Why hadn't I thought of chiropractic before?

"You practically saved my life, you know," I said, looking him in the eye.

He smiled, giving me a kind nod. "People like you are why I got into chiropractic. I make plenty of money, but the real reward comes in knowing that I made a permanent difference in your life."

"You did. You really did."

"You could be a profound influence for so many, Bill. Just think about it."

When I imagined myself adjusting someone, taking away their pain, helping them live a healthier life, a sense of purpose and pride infused my entire being. If I could help just one person in the way that Dr. Simon Tracy had helped me, I'd be fulfilled.

PASSION

Dear Bianca,

As you grow in this world and find your unique place within it, I wanted to share my thoughts and experiences with you. Life is all about learning from your mistakes, and I hope that I can guide you through some important errors I made. Growing up, I saw very clearly a separation between people who had money and people who didn't. As a result, I became obsessed with making something of myself. Early on, this equated to changing my status by making lots of money. It took me a while to discover that money wasn't the key to happiness and fulfillment.

Don't get me wrong; money is important. I read somewhere that money isn't the only thing, but it ranks right up there with oxygen. However, I'm here to share a secret with you, one many people seem blind to, but one I'll repeat to you over and over as you grow into your greatness.

If you live your life with purpose and follow your passions, money will come. However, you must stay true to that path and not chase wealth as the ultimate goal.

Now, some may push and pull you in a variety of directions. They may urge you to choose wealth over purpose. And some may try to live vicariously through you, not able to securely stand on their own two feet. You must trust what's in your heart, what's in your soul and have conviction.

Bianca, I believe strongly that we each have a gift, something only each of us can fully share with the world. Your task, your mission in life, is to discover that gift and experience the joy that comes from sharing it courageously with the world.

I wish true happiness for you. Wake up each morning and do that thing which sets your soul on fire each and every day!

Love,

Dad

FOUR

After I got back to my dorm on Sunday night, I realized there was no point in pretending I hadn't made up my mind. I'd promised myself time to consider Dr. Simon's words, but truthfully, I knew my path had been decided. I was going to study chiropractic.

For me, the decision had always been the hardest; the execution followed easily. Within six months I'd completed the requirements necessary to apply to a local and prestigious chiropractic school, which just so happened to be Dr. Simon's alma mater. No coincidence there. I liked the idea of following in my mentor's footsteps.

I continued to work hard and play hard there as well, just as I'd always done. Over the next two years, I was a decent student and got decent grades. I lapsed into a familiar pattern of partying hard and enjoy life. *Why not?* That mentality changed abruptly one Friday night when I was enjoying my fifth round of beers with some friends at a local pub.

Joey slurred his words as he said, "Who's going to the kegger tomorrow night?"

A chorus of agreement flooded the table. I shook my head. *Did they ever stop drinking?*

"Not me," I shook my head. "Not with two mid-terms looming."

"Whatever," Matt said. "I still have time."

"Yeah, well, I want to do more than just *pass*. If you wait much longer, you'll have to pull an all-nighter."

"So, who cares?" Matt asked. "Besides, it's not like anyone cares what grade you get after you graduate, right? I mean, all we're going for is the little piece of paper that says we're chiropractors."

The other two guys grunted their agreement before they started talking about the gaggle of pretty girls at the end of the bar. No one seemed interested in a debate on the merits of education. When their lewd comments abated, they each slipped into their own momentary stupor. I sat back and watched them for a moment, disgust welling up inside me.

"What are you guys going to do about precepting?" I asked quietly.

"Huh?" Joey said.

"Precepting, you know, where you intern with a licensed chiro, learn the business and prepare to go out on your own," I said, doing my best to not sound too sarcastic.

"Why would I do that?" Joey asked, with a brusque laugh. "Working my butt off for free? No thanks."

I adjusted my ball cap backwards and grimaced. "You do it for the experience."

Matt grunted and waved his hand dismissively. "There's plenty of time to get experience after we graduate. The student clinic works fine. It's all that's required. Either way, you get your degree, so who needs to precept."

The two other guys murmured similar comments under their breath. I turned to Matt and sighed. "So, you're not going to precept either?"

He shook his head. "Wasn't planning on it. Are you?"

"Yeah, of course. It's the only way to *really* learn."

Matt shrugged and said, "To each his own."

I finished my beer and took off quickly. I looked around at the bar and wondered how many hours I'd wasted there. The go-getters in our class certainly weren't at any of the tables. The top in the class didn't have the time to waste drinking. If I wanted to be better than mediocre, I'd have to make some changes.

And it had to start immediately.

FIVE

As I entered my final year of school, all I could think about was being able to work with actual patients. The student clinic was the required place to start. Once I got the experience with the mandatory number of patients, I would be allowed to apply to precept with a practicing doctor, learning the ropes with practical application. Oddly, only a small percentage of my class was pursuing that goal. There were five clinics on the campus, but only two served general outpatients. The other three were for students and employees.

The first day I walked into one of the campus clinics I met with the doctor who'd be training me. Dr. Thompson was a tall, thin man who appeared to be in his fifties. He had a ready smile with reading glasses perpetually perched at the end of his nose. Although I wouldn't be allowed to start for another week, I wanted to get my bearings. Butterflies chased around my stomach as I walked into Dr. Thompson's office. Sitting around his desk were four other students all in white lab coats.

"Hello, there," he said, looking down at his clipboard. "Are you starting today?"

I shook my head. "No, I thought I'd just introduce myself. I start next week."

"Good, good," he said. Then he waved his hands around at the other students. "Well, this will give you an idea of what you'll be doing most days."

Sitting on my butt?

All my nervous excitement deflated like a kid's balloon as I looked at the others. They looked bored out of their minds. I mumbled some sort of reply and agreed to return the following week.

Throughout the week, I pondered what I'd observed. I must have overreacted to what was probably the clinic doctor's odd sense of humor. We were there to study and learn, not to sit around all day. Laughing, I allowed myself to regain my excitement about the clinic and began to look forward to my start date.

When it came, I finished up my last class and raced back to my dorm room to change into my blue lucky tie and my freshly-ironed lab coat. When I arrived at the clinic, my shoulders slumped as I realized I'd be fourth in line. I sighed, knowing there was nothing I could have done. I couldn't have arrived sooner without skipping a class.

I sat down on the chair next to the other students and waited. And waited. After three hours passed, someone came out and said there weren't enough patients for us all to treat. So, it wasn't Dr. Thompson's joke. Extended butt time was reality.

This is ridiculous.

I was never one to just blindly follow in everyone else's footsteps. Sitting in a chair for hours was stupid. It was never going to work for me. The other students seemed to accept it, but I couldn't. The next day, I sat down with Dr. Thompson.

"What can I do?" I asked. "I can't stand wasting time."

Dr. Thompson scratched his head. "It's not like there are patients hiding in the closets. They just aren't walking in the front door in droves."

I nodded respectfully. "Too bad I just can't get experience adjusting more students. It'd be easier."

"That would be. However, as you know, you'll need to adjust other people from the community before you graduate. It's an important part of the training."

I threw my hands up in the air. "Is there *anything* else I can do to get patients?"

He thought for a moment then nodded slowly. "We have a new outreach program going on at the gym two blocks down."

"Yeah," I said, sitting up straighter.

He put his hand up. "Don't get too excited. You'll probably be sitting around a lot there, too. However, there's always a chance that you might just succeed in interesting someone in an evaluation."

"Sounds good!"

Dr. Thompson gave me instructions on what to do and say and I picked up my backpack and jogged over to the gym. He warned me that the system wasn't tried and tested yet, and that I might need to spend a lot of time explaining the basics of chiropractic.

I didn't mind. At least I wouldn't endure all that wait time.

The first day was tough. Only two people approached my table, and neither were interested. I realized I couldn't just sit back and wait for people to walk up to me. I needed to reach out—hence the term outreach.

The next day, I made a bit of a fool of myself, stumbling over my speech to various people. Despite my ineptness, I managed to improve my pitch. And I interested a few people. So, while the other students entered a lottery to determine who'd get to adjust someone or who'd sit on their butt all day, I could boast a couple more patients. And as the week rolled by, more and more people signed up to come to the clinic.

One day when I walked into the gym, my eyes were drawn to a teenage girl crumpled into her seat to the side. She was holding her blond head in her hands, looking half conscious. I could feel the pain radiating from her slight body. My heart beat a little faster as I walked to her and her mother.

The middle-aged woman next to the girl explained that her daughter, Rebecca, was only fifteen and had been plagued with headaches for years. After asking a few questions, I discovered that their family doctor had tried a series of medications, but nothing had done much to alleviate the pain. I asked the two to come in the next day for an appointment and held my breath waiting for their reply. I exhaled in relief when they agreed. This was why I chose chiropractic. I really had a good feeling that I could help Rebecca.

With the help of Dr. Thompson, I took a series of X-rays and did a complete evaluation and analysis. It was clear there was a misalignment in the upper neck putting pressure on her brain stem that could be causing her migraines.

There was a real chance I could make a permanent improvement for this young girl and that thought made me tremble with excitement. I performed the adjustment, but after Rebecca left, I wondered if it helped. I prayed that she was experiencing relief.

As the evening wore on, I felt distracted, unable to concentrate on anything else but Rebecca. Sometimes one single adjustment could make a huge impact immediately, but more often it took a few visits before a change occurred. Would she continue to come in for adjustments, so that she could truly heal?

My fingers shook as I pressed the numbers on my cell phone. Glancing at my watch, I hoped it wasn't too late to call her. I wouldn't get any sleep without knowing how my first real patient was doing. When her mother picked up the phone, my shoulders relaxed as she expressed her appreciation for my call.

"Rebecca is sleeping now. I think it's the first night in years that she didn't have a headache. I can't thank you enough!"

I was overwhelmed with gratitude, a feeling I would never forget in the years to come. I'd made an important impact in this young girl's life, which just reaffirmed I'd chosen the correct career path.

SIX

Over the following weeks I continued to visit the gym, but also waited in line to service the few clients the small clinic attracted. After my success with Rebecca, I was emboldened to reach out to more people at the gym, as well as other places I frequented. It was clear to me that I was here on this Earth to make a difference, and chiropractic gave me that opportunity.

Mid-August our school had a homecoming weekend, where many of the alumni would return to swap stories, give lectures and catch up on their continuing education credits. The local taverns were kept busy each evening, as the doctors celebrated their reunions with stories of the past and present.

Dr. Simon Tracy made a point of attending the conference every year. While joining him for a drink, a man with an athletic build and winning smile approached us. He shook Dr. Simon's hand vigorously and said, "How have you been, Si?"

"Livin' the dream," Dr. Simon replied. Then he turned to me

and added, "May I introduce Bill Samson, my young protégé?"

I accepted his equally enthusiastic handshake with a smile. "Hello, sir!"

"So, you're a future chiropractor?" he asked with a twinkle in his eye.

I laughed. "One day, I hope to be."

"Being modest?" Dr. Simon chuckled. "Bill here's in his last year. He's looking for a preceptorship."

"Well, Bill, I'm Dr. Jack Ramsey," he said, looking me up and down. "Have any interest in precepting with me?"

I couldn't believe my ears. *Did he just offer me my dream job?*

"Yes!" I said, grinning ear to ear. "I would love that."

"Well if you are Simon's boy then you must have potential," he said with a nod. "I assume you're hard-working and dedicated like him."

"Yessir, but I need to get my clinic numbers in time," I said, more to myself than him. Before I could enter a precept program, I had to work with a certain number of patients to qualify and I was only about halfway there. I just sucked into a mental calculation of what was needed.

"Well, do it!" he said in a way that told me he expected nothing less.

I immediately liked this man. "You got it!"

The next day, I did everything I could to bring in new patients to the school clinic. I also put in the required butt time to achieve my goal. Whatever it took!

Within a couple months, I was done. I immediately called Dr. Jack and could tell he was very pleased. When he said I could start the following Monday, you'd think I had won the lottery, rather than the chance to work my tail off.

Imagining the office, I pictured twin chiropractic tables side by side. I'd work at one station next to him at the other. After each session, we'd compare notes. I was fully prepared for long hours and hard work. It was all part of the process.

When I arrived Monday, Dr. Jack welcomed me warmly, showing me around the small office. He took great pride explaining every room in the clinic.

After ten minutes, he glanced absently at his watch. "It's time to huddle."

I nodded and followed along. I didn't know what a huddle was, but wasn't about to admit that on my first day. I'd find out soon enough.

He guided me to a large open room. "This will be a good opportunity to introduce you to the team!"

As soon as the meeting began, Dr. Jack announced that I would be joining their team. He introduced me to the other doctors and Susan, the office manager, who ran the schedule and guided patients through their visit.

I sat back and listened to the three doctors discuss their patients. Everyone was taking notes, following along. Joyce needed extra care, as she had just suffered a rear end collision. A few patients were up for reminders for their monthly payments and Tom was due for a follow up exam and X-ray. They had a lot of patients and Dr. Jack was careful to make sure everyone knew what to do. I made a mental note to bring a notebook next time.

The office ran like a fine-oiled machine. This wasn't an office of silos, where everyone worked on their own and kept quiet. No, this office communicated! Anyone with any kind of concern could voice it during the huddle and by the end, the entire team was clued in on what was going on.

I vowed to run my practice that way one day.

Nervous energy coursed through my frame as Dr. Jack addressed me. "And Dr. Bill, we're so glad to have you on board! We really need your help. Dr. Lorenzo here is going to show you our chiropractic software."

I nodded and looked to Dr. Lorenzo, who grimaced and shook his head slightly.

Did he just give me a pitying look?

No matter. I was willing to do what was required to learn how to run a successful office. Determined to do my best, I followed Dr. Lorenzo into a small room, which resembled a broom closet.

Still excited and ready to learn every aspect of the business, I soon discovered that this particular task involved learning all about the wonders of mind-numbing data entry.

Brutal!

My enthusiasm waned as I worked to catch up on all the three doctors' handwritten notes. One by one, I entered them into the software and follow up with various insurance companies who were behind on payments. They were seriously behind on this work.

This is seriously what I'm doing? I railed.

Well at least I'll learn this for my office, I reasoned.

This is ridiculous, I complained internally.

The work was so tedious, it drained me completely. When I'd get home all I could do was slump into my favorite chair and watch whatever happened to be on television. Had my classmates had been right? Maybe they had chosen to steer clear of precepting, because they'd truly understood what was involved.

After a week, Dr. Jack pulled me aside. "Why the long face?"

I didn't want him to think badly of me, so I just said, "Sorry."

"No need to apologize. I just want to know what's going on."

I shrugged. "It's nothing."

He studied me for a moment then said, "I know data entry isn't the most exciting work in the world. But I have a reason for asking you to do it, you know. You're going to have to know how to run an office from soup to nuts. If you let the patient files get disorganized, you'll get really bogged down."

I nodded, realizing that he was right. "True."

"Look, we just got this software and it's state of the art. I'm training you on this, so you don't have to go through all the headaches I did with the handwritten notes. I think you can see how much of a nightmare that would have been."

I nodded and stopped feeling sorry for myself. It occurred to me that I needed this experience every bit as much as I'd need to learn about the human body. Because of Dr. Jack Ramsey's diligence, I now was trained in something that other students didn't have a clue about—how to handle the files of a small clinic.

When I walked into Dr. Jack's clinic the following day, I had a different attitude. I joined the huddle like a new man. As we discussed all the patients arriving that day, I realized that I knew the particulars about each patient and could contribute worthwhile information.

I had become part of the team without adjusting a single patient.

SEVEN

That week, Dr. Jack started training me on basic office protocols over the lunch breaks. He gave me tools to help me communicate with patients in a variety of circumstances. We practiced specific wording to patients for initial exams, reports on findings, etc. This gave me an inner feeling of comfort and security, as I could really connect with patients for the first time.

It took time to learn what to say well enough to make it my own. We practiced different scenarios over and over and when I could be completely natural, Dr. Jack allowed me to start giving some face-to-face preliminary exams.

I started with a new patient exam, which was the first opportunity to make a great impression as the old expression goes. When patients came in, I took the time to really get to know them. I wrote down his or her history and took care of the various testing needed, which would help formulate a diagnosis and determine if X-rays were needed. I did my best to develop a relationship with the patient through the exam, hoping that they would come back the next day for their report of findings.

Dr. Jack was careful to explain to me that from day one we must not only treat their physical concerns, but also compassionately find out how it has affected them mentally.

"Treat the person, not just the condition," was one of his favorite expressions.

Once I completed my evaluation, I would review my findings with Dr. Jack and he would go in and speak with the patient. As I watched him work with people, I observed that the more important the patient felt, the more likely they would be to follow our recommendations. It was a rewarding step to learn.

A few weeks later, Susan began a two-week vacation and my training took a new direction. I can honestly say I was less than thrilled when I was asked to step in and take over her responsibilities.

I'm a doctor, not a front desk manager.

Boy had I failed to appreciate her vital role! That was a mistake I would never make again.

Susan trained me on everything I'd need to know. She taught me how to enter patients into the system, check them in and out, bill them, handle insurance, phone calls and, of course, always greet and say goodbye to every patient.

Whenever possible, I would talk to leading business people and try to glean what they did to achieve success. One for one, they all agreed that "Hellos" and "Goodbyes" were vital. Those moments of kindness stay with people.

The minute Susan left, I felt swallowed up by all the responsibilities. To say I was slow would be putting it nicely. I made sure to smile, but my attention was just on keeping up with the flurry of activity. I couldn't do much else.

Dr. Jack noticed my struggles, "Bill, I don't care if you fall behind with the paperwork, that's OK. You can always catch up after shift," he reassured me, putting his hand on my shoulder. "Just, please, don't forget that greetings and send-offs are the most important part of this position."

Something that Dr. Jack said that stuck with me was that with any product or service, all it takes is one bad experience for the customer to lose interest and devalue you. Focus on great service, make the customers feel special and they would keep coming back.

So, I upped my game. I focused more on the patients and kept Dr. Jack's words in mind. However, I soon discovered some patients were more challenging than others.

Mr. Teaver was an elderly patient, who came in twice a week. He barely looked at me when he came up to reception. Then he'd always grumble his answers to my questions. I found myself tensing up when he walked in the door; I dreaded seeing his name on the schedule. He didn't seem to care too much for anyone.

So, why bother?

I just wasn't interested in my lasting impressions with Mr. Teaver. Then something changed after I'd been running reception for a week. I'd discovered my groove and finally felt the front desk was my territory, like I was welcoming people into my home. It took me a while, but I finally realized that hospitality was not merely about having good manners. It was the difference between a patient having an OK experience or a great one. My job was to make sure their experience was so good they would talk about it to their friends.

It was at that moment that I decided to play a game with myself. I was going to do everything I could to improve Mr. Teaver's mood. What's the worst that could happen? I was going to win him over or just piss him off. I was oddly fine with either outcome. I knew it wouldn't happen overnight, but if I was genuine with him and really focused my attention on him, maybe I could help to turn things around.

The next time he came in, I took a beat and relaxed my shoulders which had naturally tensed up. I looked at him, gave him a smile and said, "Well, good morning, Mr. Teaver. Great to see you today. Is there anything I can do for you?"

He looked at the counter in front of me and grumbled, "No."

I nodded, giving him a smile, despite the fact he wasn't looking at me. People can sense a smile. Even over the phone, people can hear it in your voice.

"Well, Dr. Jack will be with you in a few minutes," I said.

I watched him sit, and pick up a gardening magazine. Since he wasn't just thumbing through it, I gathered he had a genuine interest in the articles. After ten minutes, he went back to get an adjustment and on his way out, I gave him a cheerful goodbye. His response was a curt grunt before he left.

Next time, I thought. *Game on.*

When he returned in two days, I greeted his scowling face with another smile. He responded with a grumble. I tensed in irritation, but quickly shook it off instead. It wasn't the right way to respond.

I figured I had no way of knowing what was going on in his life.

Maybe he was dealing with a difficult situation at home or work. Maybe he just hated being old. Either way, it was my mission to break down Mr. Teaver's forcefield. My goal became defined: to get him to smile!

Here goes nothing.

I took a deep breath and blurted out, "My mother has had a garden in her backyard ever since I was little."

As the words came out of my mouth I realized it probably sounded like it came out of nowhere. What did gardening have to do with this clinic?

Except I knew *this* patient liked gardening. I needed to find *some* common ground with Mr. Teaver, something we could share, if just for a moment. So, I continued on. I told him about how we always had fresh vegetables on the table, even when times were tough and how I'd always appreciated that.

His head lifted and when I captured his blue eyes with mine for just a moment, I caught his small smile. And in that instant, I wasn't invisible to him anymore. He'd truly acknowledged my existence. Then the moment passed and he dropped his head, found his chair and picked up another magazine.

In anticipation of his visit, I'd dug around the office and picked out all the gardening magazines to fan out on the mahogany table. I couldn't tell if he noticed, as he didn't say a word. But I had to think on some level, it must have registered with him. He went back to see Dr. Jack and left without saying a word.

The next time he came in, I gave him a warm smile and he responded with a nod in my direction. Then, on his way out of the office, he tipped his hat, glanced my way and said, "See ya, Bill."

If he'd plopped down a Benjamin Franklin on the front desk and said, "Here's a tip. Thanks," I don't think I could have been more stunned or more pleased. It took me a moment to find my tongue, but I finally managed to stutter out a stunned farewell as he walked out.

LOVE

Dear Bianca,

I have two words to share with you, my daughter. Two words that I've learned make all the difference in this world, two words that are key for success and will assure you stand out.

Love and kindness.

As you grow, I encourage you to strive to be the person that treats others with love and kindness, pure and simple. Now, it won't always be easy, because people will try your patience. Sometimes, they'll be moody and negative, challenging and difficult. Don't give up on them. Instead, continue to go above and beyond, roll up your sleeves and work hard, doing everything you can to help each person you meet. Whenever I make a decision, using my heart, I am rewarded with a feeling of courage.

Let me share something fascinating I learned. The Latin root for courage is cor, which means heart. To be courageous, you must not only have love in your heart, but you must love what you do. It's all part of the essence of the word and will ultimately lead to your fulfillment.

Looking around, you'll notice that people make decisions based on fear and love. I'm sad to say that most pick fear. Bianca, please choose love and fight through the fear. Oh, make no mistake, you'll have times of fear, there's no way around that. It's just a fact of life. However, if you have the courage to fight through your fears you will be able to rise above them and succeed. Consistently do this and you'll discover that you can actually use fear as a catalyst to push you through. The struggle is what will give you strength. Just never allow fear to cripple you or keep you from your dreams and passions, like so many people do.

Bianca, if you go above and beyond, with whatever you do, it will not only make a huge impression on others, but you will succeed in building your own self-image. After all, that's the essence of self-esteem, and is the origin of self-confidence. When you choose love, and go the extra mile for others, you'll always stand out as the courageous leader we all can be.

Love,

Dad

EIGHT

By the time Susan's two weeks were up, I felt comfortable sitting behind the front desk. Still, when she walked in the door wearing a flower lei, her face a toasty brown, I felt relief. I gave her a broad smile and said, "Welcome home."

She glanced at the reception area and gave a nod of approval. "Looks like you have things under control. Maybe I should hit the Caribbean next."

I laughed, shaking my head. "Let's not get carried away, Susan."

"Last time we had a trainee run my front desk, they left it a mess. Poor kid was a nervous wreck by the time I came back."

I shrugged, "Dr. Jack helped out."

As if on cue, Dr. Jack walked up and gave me a shoulder pat. "Bill, I think you're ready to shift gears."

I did an internal happy dance as I followed him down the corridor. This was it! I was going to finally adjust people. I mentally rolled up my sleeves and considered all the patients on the books for that week. Which would be mine?

"You're going to learn about marketing now!" he said with his usual enthusiasm.

The walls of the hallway started to cave in on me, as the floor threatened to swallow me up. "What?" I snapped before I had time to reel the word back into my mouth. "I...I mean, what?"

"Son, marketing is the most important job of the business, any business really."

"Yeah, but..." *I hate sales. Hate with a fiery passion.*

"To thrive you must be able to get people in the door. If you're good at marketing and sales, trust me, you'll do well. It's important." Dr. Jack suddenly reminded me of a used car salesman trying to get rid of the last lemon on the lot.

This is B.S., I thought, but I nodded dutifully and quietly said, "OK."

Dr. Jack shook his head. "Bill, why did you get into chiropractic?"

"To help people," I said. *And make money*, I added to myself.

"Good! Now, if you want to share your hard-earned knowledge with others, you'll need to do so one person at a time. There's no way around that."

"Except if you do lectures," I said, perking up. "Then you can get in front of many."

"Sure, and that's a great plan! But in the end, you'll find that you still need to sit down with Joe and Jane, individually, to really reach them. People need that one on one connection before they commit."

I slumped against the wall and nodded. He was right. It made sense. "OK, so how do I go about learning marketing?"

Dr. Jack nodded with a relieved smile. "I'll set it up. You'll tag along with Dr. Lorenzo to a car show on Wednesday. That's a good place to start."

"A *car show?*" I asked. *You've got to be kidding me!*

He chuckled. "Yeah, I know. Sounds pretty weird. Believe it or not, it's great training. You'll see! It's a good way to get in front of a bunch of people."

So, the following Wednesday, Dr. Lorenzo and I went down to a local car show after the clinic closed its doors. People were milling around, chatting, interested in the fancy cars that were scattered around the fairgrounds and the beer was flowing like oil through an engine. Dr. Lorenzo and I had a table off to one side, where we attempted to schedule new patient appointments. We set up a long mirror next to the small folding table, so that people could check out their posture. I felt like a tuxedo salesman at a cat expo.

Now, I knew my stuff, because I'd drilled it. I could repeat it all back in my sleep without any trouble. But, here I was, out of my element, surrounded by a bunch of tipsy car enthusiasts, checking out automobiles I could only afford in my wildest dreams. At best these people were vaguely amused with my pitch, but deep down I worried that they considered me a joke.

Despite all my concerns and doubts, I did my best, belting enthusiasm with each and every presentation. However, it was all for nothing. No one signed up for an appointment.

What's wrong with these people?

Quite a few had a look that reminded me of captured prey, waiting for the first chance to turn tail and run. Some did try to hide their yawns, while others gave me a glazed look with vacant nods. Overall, the whole experience was a bust, just like I knew it would be.

The next day, Dr. Jack gave me a huge smile. "How did it go yesterday?"

"Horrible," I confessed.

"What do you think happened?"

"Honestly?" I said with a shake of my head. "I think it's the venue. They were there to see cars, not talk to me. And most were tipsy."

He put an arm around my shoulder. "Let's talk over lunch. Let's see if we can figure this out."

I nodded and watched him walk away. I didn't think there was much he could say. The more I thought about it, the more it seemed painfully obvious that pitching chiropractic treatments at a car show wasn't a brilliant idea. The problem had nothing to do with me, it was the quality of prospects that was the problem. When I got together with Dr. Jack I explained that to him.

He shook his head. "A failure at sales has little to do with the prospect. It's never their fault. It always comes down to the salesman."

"But how do you explain their lack of interest?"

"Tell me exactly what happened. What did you say, then what did they say? Give it to me straight."

I took a deep breath and launched into my ten-minute explanation of the human body. I put all my heart and soul into it, gesturing for emphasis. I did my best to impress Dr. Jack, as I had the prospect, with my knowledge and expertise.

Dr. Jack cut me off half way through with a wave of his hand. "I see the problem."

Puzzled, as I hadn't gotten the good part, I asked, "You do?" I was just getting going.

He smiled gently at me. "You're talking too much."

What was he talking about? "But, how am I supposed to motivate them to set an appointment if I don't educate?"

"Well," he said, "do you feel they were listening to you or were their eyes sort of glossed over?"

I looked at him and sighed. "They were tuned out."

"Right. And if they're tuning out, they're not listening. That means you're just wasting your breath."

"Huh," I grunted, looking away for a moment. I had to admit he was right about that. In my gut, I knew they hadn't truly appreciated my words, my wisdom, my knowledge. "OK then, what should I do?"

"Well, start by listening. And throw out the big words."

"But, how I am I supposed to impress anyone if I don't let them know I know what I'm talking about? I mean, doesn't medical terminology impress people?"

"No one cares about how smart you are!" Dr. Jack said emphatically. "Why do you think they are sitting there, listening?"

That got me thinking. I stopped pacing and sat down. My head swirled with possible answers, but then the truth finally hit me. I looked up at him and said, "To see if I can help them."

"Exactly!" he said. "They stopped at your table. Why? Because they're hoping you might be able to make their life better, somehow. That's the only reason people stop."

I nodded. Somehow, I'd missed that point.

"And really, that's the only reason they're listening to you at all. You've got to stop trying to *impress* people. It'll just confuse them."

I folded my arms across my chest, "So, what do I do then?"

"You *listen*."

We spent the next few lunch breaks drilling that concept. I learned to weave my pitch into my answers to the questions they asked.

Dr. Jack helped me learn the art of brevity. "Why use nine words when four will do?" he liked to say.

So, I learned to listen. I also tossed all the fancy medical terms and stuck with words that most people understood. As a result, I realized I sounded more like the kind of person I'd want to talk to, someone I would trust. I knew I was on the right track.

The following Wednesday, I applied everything I'd learned and resisted the urge to resort to talking the prospect's ear off. I really focused on listening to the prospect in front of me. Many were still disinterested, but one middle-aged man seemed eager to chat.

The minute he walked into my area, I knew I liked him. There was just something about him. "What's your name?" I asked.

"George Thurman."

"Well, Mr. George," I said with a smile, following the pattern the office used of using a person's first name. Dr. Jack always said that it was a good step toward bringing a person into our family of patients. "You look like you want to tell me something?"

I noticed he was rubbing his lower back, but refrained from

pointing it out. It was far better to get him to tell me what was going on—in his own words.

"It's my lower back. It hurts, a lot," he groaned. "And it seems to be getting worse."

I could hear Dr. Jack's words echo in my ear, *Remember, it's about them, not you.* So, I said, "What do you think caused it?"

"Aside from being fat and lazy? I have no idea."

I gave him a crooked smile. "When is it the worst?"

"Toward the end of the day."

I nodded. "What do you do for work?"

"Insurance," he replied. "I sit in a cubicle all day, handling claims on the phone.

I continued to nod, mentally noting that most people hunch over their desks in that situation, which is murder on their lower back. My mouth opened to launch into a thirty-minute dissertation on the evils of a sedentary lifestyle, but closed it again. He just wanted help, not a lecture.

"So, you feel the pain when you get home?" I asked.

He nodded. "Yeah, mostly."

"What happens then?"

He thought for a moment. "Jessie and Sam chase around me the moment I get home."

"They your kids?"

"Yeah."

"And you pick them up?"

"I wish I could," he lamented. "But I can't. All I can do is reach down and give them a hug. But even that hurts. I hate it."

My heart went out to him. "I can imagine. Here, you work hard all day long, for them. Then when you get a chance to be with your children, you're in pain. That's rough!"

He looked me in the eye, his eyes widening. "You get it! That's exactly right. I'd give anything to be able to pick up my kids and play with them. Even for a bit!"

"Well, George, I have some good news for you. We might be able to help you achieve that goal."

"How?"

As I studied him, I had no doubt that he was interested. Really interested. Now, with that crucial ingredient in place, I could give him a little education.

George became my first new patient and, with Dr. Jack's help, we got him started on a program that would ultimately allow him to pick up his children and be an active father.

That day, I hated sales a little less.

NINE

"I can't stand sales," I groaned, as I sat at my mother's dining table a month later, devouring the last of my mother's chicken pot pie on my plate. "All those *no's* just get to me."

"Tell me about it," my brother said. "I have the same problem. Try door to door sales sometime. It is rough."

I shook my head. "I can only imagine. And don't get me started on all the people who promise to come to the office, but don't."

Mom dished out a second portion of pot pie, then sat down. "What do you mean?"

Frustration bubbled up inside me. "It's just that so many people say they'll come in for an exam then no show."

"Well, now, what do *you* do to make sure they come in?" she asked.

"Hm?" I inquired absently, as I scooped another forkful of chicken into my mouth.

She put a gentle hand on my shoulder. "You're complaining that people say they'll come visit, but don't. Do I have it right?"

I nodded.

"So, my question is—what are *you* doing about it?"

I furrowed my brows. "What can *I* do? Nothing. People are flakes."

Even as the words came out of my mouth, I thought of Dr. Jack words: *A failure at sales has little to do with the prospect. It's never their fault. It always comes down to the salesman.*

"Have you tried following up?" she asked.

I shook my head. "Not sure there's any point in that."

"Of course, there is!" she said heatedly.

I groaned, as my shoulders slumped. I knew that tone. I was disappointing Mom and that was never a good thing. I lowered my fork to the plate and gave her my full attention. "OK."

She shook her head. "Son, you care about all the people you talk to. Don't you? I know you do."

I nodded. "Of course."

"Why did you put all those hours in on your finals? I saw all the books you brought home. You're always working. So, tell me, why are you working so hard?"

I looked her in the eye. "To help people."

"Well, you need to show that attitude to everyone you talk to! They need to feel that you're not just interested in them for the moment. They want to be reassured that you'll help them long term. Following up does that. Trust me, if you follow up with folks, you'll get more patients."

I realized she was right. It wouldn't be hard to call people the day before the appointment. At least I'd know they wouldn't forget. "I'll try that."

"I'll tell you, that's what I do any time I want people to show up for a church social. And those are free!" she said leaning back in her chair. "People need reminders. They're busy with a lot of competing pressures hitting them from all sides."

Over the next few weeks, I let all the prospects know that I'd be calling them the day before their scheduled appointments. Then I made sure to follow through on my promise. Mom was right. More people came in.

I still felt like banging my head against the wall from all the *no's* I was getting. Most people just weren't interested in talking to me, opening up, and sharing their health issues. Dr. Jack saw my discouraged face one day and suggested I branch out and try a few more venues.

The stormy look I gave him made him laugh. "What's your biggest problem?" he asked.

"Pretty much everyone says some version of 'No, thank you.' I'm sick of it! I hate the rejection."

"Don't take it so personally," he said. "They aren't really rejecting *you*, you know."

"It feels like they are," I muttered.

"Yeah, you've got to get over that and fast. Heck, they don't know you well enough to feel one way or the other about you," he said with a chuckle.

That's true. His words were logical, but I couldn't get around the fact that it felt like I'd been sucker punched every time I put myself out there and got hit with a *no*. It was just discouraging.

"Just remember it's a number's game," he said. When he saw my deflated expression, he laughed. "Yeah, I know you've heard that before, but it's true. The fact is you just have to get in front of a certain number of people to make a sale."

"How many?" I asked.

"Now that's the real question, isn't it?" he said with a nod. "You'll figure that out. It will be different for you than it will for me. And it will be different with each venue. It really depends on your marketing campaign as well as various factors. There's no pat answer.

"I'll give you an example. My brother-in-law is a landscaper. He likes to canvas an area with flyers. Mind you, he's been doing this for some time and has it down to a science, but he'll tell you that if he puts a hundred and fifty flyers out on doors he'll get one call in."

My mouth hung open. "It's that predictable?"

"Sure," he said. "It's just numbers, that's all."

"But everyone who calls won't sign up with him," I said, thinking out loud, "so, does he know how many people calling in will turn into clients?"

"Actually, yes, he does," Dr. Jack said. "Roughly a quarter."

"So..." I said, mentally calculating, "he'll need to put out six hundred flyers to get one actual client."

"Bingo!" Dr. Jack said approvingly.

"That's a lot of flyers."

"Not really, not when you consider that people usually hire him for the long term. Once a person has a gardener, they don't usually want to switch."

"True."

"And he'd tell you that he likes the exercise. It takes him two mornings to get out six hundred flyers:

"That's not bad," I said with a low whistle. "And he's doing pretty well?"

"Marketing is part of his daily routine, so he's always expanding. Right now he's got three crews in the field."

"So, I guess I just have to figure out how many people I need to approach to get a *yes*," I murmured. "OK, you're right. I need more sites to set up at. Any ideas?"

"Think outside the box. I mean you could go to wellness expos, but you'll have competition. It's worth a try, but I'd suggest finding a venue that isn't health related. Just use your noggin and come up with places where you'll be the only health care professional."

I thought about it and scoured the internet for events happening within a fifteen-mile radius. There wasn't a shortage of opportunities, which was a blessing. I gave bridal expos a try and had some success.

Finals came and went and I graduated with honors, making my mother cry. She kept telling me how proud she was of me and how I was carving a new path for our family, one my children could follow.

I was generally feeling good and was getting some traction. My pitch had definitely improved and I was starting to build some steam. If I went to two events a week, I'd get twenty new people signing up for a new patient visit. Then when I followed up with each of them, half would usually show up to that first appointment. Then six of those would actually continue with a program. So, two events a week would yield six actual patients.

Eager to keep the momentum going, I branched out into various venues that didn't have competition. One event that sounded promising was a middle-of-the-day wine tasting event a few blocks down from the clinic. I was excited when I stepped outside and saw the sun shining. I predicted that people would be in a good mood and they'd be properly lubricated, so maybe, just maybe, they'd be open to my offer for an evaluation.

Most people were really nice and relaxed, thanks to the wine. That made things easier. During a lull toward the end of the day I was mentally calculating all the appointments I'd get as a result of the day's efforts. I was grinning when a skinny blond lady with wire rimmed glasses came by the table.

"Who are you?" she bit out.

I started to answer her, telling her about what I was doing when she cut me off. "I don't care who you are!"

My eyes flickered toward various people who had turned to stare in our direction. I could feel my cheeks getting hot. I'd never encountered anything like her before. All I could seem to do was stand there and stare at her.

"How can you disgrace yourself like this?" she snarled.

I wanted to walk away, but I couldn't. I wished I could ignore her, but that wasn't possible either. No, all I could do was stand there and take her rising and irrational anger. Finally, the only thing I could say was, "I'm not disgracing myself."

"You sure are!" she said with a biting laugh. "You're belittling your profession by sitting here in the middle of a wine tasting event. *What* are you thinking?"

My hands clenched and unclenched by my sides, as I did my

best to control my temper. I was well aware of the growing number of eyes on us and I had to keep my cool. "I'm just here—"

She waved her hand, interrupting and said, "Why can't you just get patients the *normal* way? It's people like you that give chiropractors a bad name!"

She continued to assail me with a barrage of insults, getting louder and louder. With each rude comment, I felt more and more boxed in, helpless and trapped. There was just nothing I could do to stop the words from spilling into the space. Finally, she ended her tirade with, "What do you have to say for yourself?"

I sighed heavily. "Ma'am, I'm just trying to help people. That's why I'm here." I knew my words were falling on deaf ears, but I had to try to defend myself. Besides I'd hoped the eavesdroppers might appreciate my sentiment.

For some reason, my words made her stop shouting at me. She just stood there for a moment, staring at me. I guess she didn't have any ammo left in her. After a few minutes, she shook her head and left, pulling her poor husband along with her. I imagine that she probably continued her rant as she trailed out to the parking lot.

For a good five minutes, I stood rooted from the assault. I did my best to calm nerves and stop my head from spinning out of control. I felt like I'd been pummeled by a vicious category five hurricane. As soon as I could, I packed up and left, carefully avoiding looking anyone in the eye.

TEN

All the way home, I could hear the angry woman's words echoing in my ears as if she were in the passenger seat. I kept trying to think of different things I could have said, clever retorts or snappy comebacks, but nothing came to mind. I was plagued with the thought that maybe she was right. Maybe I was in fact demeaning my profession.

When I arrived home, I called Dr. Lorenzo. He patiently listened to the story then sighed. "Yeah, I've gotten that before."

By the time I hung up, I felt a little better. The next day, Dr. Jack came over to me and said, "A little bird told me that things didn't go too well yesterday."

I shook my head. "That's putting it mildly."

"So, the question is, what are you going to do now?"

I looked him in the eye. "I'm not going to let that lady stop me. I still got five confirms for the day, despite her."

"Right!" he said. "That's pretty good. Look, there will always be hecklers out there, people trying to stop you for one reason or another. It's the way of the world."

"How do you handle it?"

"I try to help them. After all, they're part of my mission as well. Your ultimate success will come down to how you respond to situations like the one you had to deal with yesterday."

I nodded, considering his words. "That's makes sense."

"So, are you going to the next wine tasting event Thursday?"

"You bet!" I said. I felt a burst of renewed energy course through me. That experience had been a challenge, nothing more. And I'd have plenty of opportunities to handle other angry people, no doubt. I just needed to find a way to help them.

The next event started smoothly. I talked to a few dozen people, all polite, and I was feeling more relaxed. However, about half way through the event an older guy approached my table. Despite being a few feet from me, he belted out, "So, you wanna crack my bones?"

At first, I didn't know what to say. Was he serious?

He didn't give me time to respond. He just looked me in the eye and said, "Is that what you wanna do?" He then looked around at the bustling room and boomed out, "Hey, this guy wants to crack my bones!"

The guy's voice carried well across the open space. Several people turned to give me a cautious and careful look. I would have thought he was drunk, but his words were cleared not slurred.

At least he's not angry!

After the encounter from the previous week I was mentally prepared for this guy. I took a deep breath and thought, *Ok, I know exactly what I'm going to say. And I'm going to say it with love in my heart*. I made sure that I didn't feel any anger or irritation when I replied.

I took a deep breath and said, "No, sir, I don't wanna crack your bones. I wanna improve your health and healing. I wanna preserve and restore optimal health to your body. I want to help make sure that you enjoy playing with your kids and your children's kids, for as long as you live. That's what I want to do, sir. Now are you interested in an evaluation?"

After I stopped talking, the guy just stared at me. He was very quiet, so I just continued to look at him, being open to him. I felt genuine affection for him and I wanted to help him with every fiber of my being. I willed him to listen to my words and recognize that I cared for him.

The pause lengthened then he finally nodded. "Oh, well now, how are you gonna do that?"

Relief flooded through me as if a dam had been released. I grinned widely and said, "Come over here and I'll tell you."

And with that, he allowed me to explain all about how the nervous system worked, the brain-body connection and everything else I needed to explain in order to get him to comprehend what I could do for him.

After a little time, he agreed to come in the following Monday to the office. I knew that he'd sign on for treatment, because he *got* my message. He really *got* it. It was at that moment I realized that sometimes the hardest struggles can turn into the greatest victories.

Looking back, if I'd allowed that first lady to crush me, I might have canceled further outreach programs. I was so glad that I hadn't.

Instead, I'd pushed through. And as a result, I was stronger and more resolved and more able to help others.

Every patient who came in, was another person whose life could be improved. If I didn't firmly believe that, I couldn't continue to market and sell. Fear would well inside me still, but I learned to move through it.

I improved and so did the clinic. Dr. Jack responded by making a few enhancements. One involved a new piece of equipment, a special thermography scanner, which was run with a handheld device and a personal computer. As a result, we could show people increased levels of heat in their body. This was an important tool that helped educate patients about what was going on with their bodies, so they'd become more engaged and interested in healing themselves.

In addition, Dr. Jack gave me a greater allowance for additional outreach programs. He authorized me to go to more and more trade shows. After a few months he called me into his office one day.

"Bill, you're doing great. I mean it. I'm impressed!"

"Thanks," I said, feeling proud that my mentor had noticed my hard work.

"Have a seat," he said, indicating a chair next to him. "I've been meaning to talk to you."

"I've got a bridal expo in an hour," I said, glancing at my watch as I sat down.

"That's fine," he said with a wave of a hand. "I want to start by asking what you've learned about sales."

"Hm?" I asked.

"You're on a roll," he said. "Every time you go out, you come back with quite a few new scheduled patients. I just wondered what you feel accounts for your success."

I pursed my lips and thought. "Well," I said. "It comes down to a few things. They have to like you. I think that's where it starts. If the person you're talking to doesn't like you, it's not going anywhere."

Dr. Jack nodded. "Go on."

"They have to trust you, too."

"Good!" he said. "And how do you get them to trust you so fast?"

"Uh..." I didn't know how to answer that. They just did. They trusted me because...*why*? It occurred to me that I didn't really know.

"What are you doing to create trust?" he prompted.

"Well, I *care*," I said. "And they seem to know that."

He nodded. "But, how? How do they know?"

"Well, I listen, for one."

"Bingo!" Dr. Jack said, slapping his knee with his hand. "That's exactly right. You listen—and you honestly care. There's no doubt in my mind that the people you bring in can see that. My guess is that you stopped talking and talking, and started really hearing them. Am I right?"

"Yeah!"

"You learned to keep quiet a bit. Didn't you?"

"Yeah," I said with a grin. "I guess I did."

"And that brings us to where I'm going with this. I want to give you a promotion. I want to bring you into the next phase of our business model, where you can educate people properly."

My adrenaline soared when he said the word "promotion." *I was really being promoted?* "Wow, that's great!"

"Anyone can be enormously successful, Bill. Anyone. It really takes two things. Number one, you've got to get in front of people. And you're doing that. In spades! Continue to do what you're doing. Some sales people, well they start getting comfortable or something. They stop reaching out to new people and guess what happens?"

"They stop making sales."

"Exactly. Makes sense. Right?"

"So," I puzzled through this. "Does that mean you want me to continue to market?"

Dr. Jack nodded. "Yeah. You can't drop that. It's working. Keep it up. No, we're going to add something. That's the second thing I mentioned. You have to go the extra mile, care enough about the person to make sure they follow through and sign up for the treatments. To do that, you need to be able to deal with objections. You need to learn to close people."

"Oh," I said, as all the built-up excitement drained from me in a manner of seconds. What was Dr. Jack pitching now? More sales?

He must have noticed my less than enthusiastic response, because he shook his head. "Look, Bill, I never said this would be easy, right? It isn't. It all takes a lot of hard work and you need to learn a lot of stuff before you can make it."

"Yeah, I'm getting that. I guess a college degree isn't enough."

"Don't get me wrong, the degree you earned is important and necessary, but that's not where your education ends. That's why you signed up for precepting before you graduated. And that's why you're here—with me. You're willing to roll up your sleeves to be a success. I really respect that."

I frowned. "It's just right when I think I have things down, I'm hit with the fact that I don't really know enough. There always seems to be more to learn."

Dr. Jack rested his hand on my shoulder. "I'm still learning. We all are. When you stop learning new things, you might as well give up, because you're done."

I looked at him and nodded. I felt a bit better. "OK."

"You're a go-getter, Bill. That's the reason I am investing so much in you. I believe you have what it takes. But mark my words, there's no magic pill. Nothing that will instantly rocket you up to the top of your field. There's only one thing, one thing that will make a difference. You know what that is?"

I nodded and gulped hard. "Hard work."

"You said it!"

EMPATHY

Dear Bianca,

People often ask me, "What is the key to true success?" The answer is very simple. It's all about people. Remember, there is only so much you can do on your own. You need to inspire others, so that people will want to work with you.

One thing I've learned the hard way is that people and sales are basically synonymous. I know, I know, you might have the idea that sales is evil. You wouldn't be alone in that thought! The fact is that when I first started, I told myself, I'm not a sales person. I'm a doctor! Well, I quickly learned that if you're in a business, and you need to communicate a message, you're in sales.

Sales isn't about persuading a large number of people to do things they don't want to do or shouldn't do. No, it's really about leading them. And to do that, it comes down to you and the rapport you develop with others. Sales has nothing to do with how smart you sound, speeches loaded with technobabble. The only thing that matters is that people know that you have their best interests at heart and truly care about them.

I can whittle the aspects of sales into three simple steps, three things you must accomplish when selling (I learned this from your Papa):

1. People must like you.
2. They must trust you.
3. You must teach them something. (or allow them to see the solution for themselves)

And please remember, before you can touch anyone, you need to really listen to them. Listen to the person in front of you and be fully present. Then, you can better serve them, and deliver a response that resonates with them. That, my daughter, is the essence of sales.

Love,
Dad

ELEVEN

Damned if I felt a little like I was a frosh again. I realized I was getting better at tackling a new area, though. I guess *that* was something. And I felt good that I'd somewhat mastered the initial patient visit. So, now I was moving onto the "report of findings."

In our office, the second visit was divided into three parts. The first step involved a group orientation, which was held two or three times a week, depending upon the need. Dr. Jack would deliver a thirty-minute discussion on the patient's role in their own healthcare.

Through this lecture, each participant learned how to read and analyze an X-ray. They'd immediately put this knowledge to use in the next segment, the breakout section. To segue between the two parts, Dr. Jack would engage them with an emotional close.

Dr. Jack would share a personal and intimate story with the people there. He always took a seat for this part, and lowered his voice to really communicate to the participants. He was so sincere as he shared about the debilitating headaches he had suffered throughout his childhood.

None of the medical doctors could help. All they suggested were drugs, which he'd refused to take. It was when he ran into a chiropractor at the gym that his life turned around. Each orientation participant could feel his joy, relief and astonishment when he was finally pain free. Each time I heard Dr. Jack's story, I could feel his newfound freedom. I never grew tired of hearing his story. It was powerful.

So, by the time the prospects were done with the introductory lecture, they were ready for a one-on-one, in-depth discussion. Dr. Jack allowed me to sit in on these. I immediately noticed that people tended to sit on the edge of their chairs as Dr. Jack showed them their individual X-rays.

Because he'd taken the time to properly educate them, they knew what to look for, and they could actually read their own X-rays. Since they'd been educated in what a healthy spine should look like, they could immediately notice problems with theirs and know the effect those problems would cause for them.

Dr. Jack believed in keeping patients in the driver's seat by asking questions, rather than explain everything to the person again.

Say he'd put up a film of the patient's lower back. He'd often start with, "OK, what do you see, Mrs. Anne?"

Then she might say, "I have a curvature of my lower back." See, she diagnosed her condition, not Dr. Jack.

"Right!" he'd say with an approving nod. "So, now, what do you think that might be doing to you?"

"It's compressing my spine."

"And what's that doing?" he'd prompt.

"Huh, that's why I have pain in my leg!" She'd smile, because she understood what was going on with her body, maybe for the first time in her life. "That's causing my sciatica!"

"Bravo," Dr. Jack would say. Once he'd got a patient to properly diagnose their issue, he'd reinforce everything they'd discussed in the earlier lecture, which was now more relatable to them.

This was such a crucial step, because if the prospect didn't have their epiphany, they wouldn't close well. They wouldn't see the importance of investing in their own health. That's why Dr. Jack worked hard to get them to become their *own* doctor.

Each of these two steps, the intro lecture and the one-on-one, took time. It wasn't wise to short cut it. I think that's true for almost any profession. If you're selling property or selling cars, you need to take the time to educate the person in front of you fully, ensuring they're part of the team. If you find they are just nodding their head while you talk, you've lost them.

At the end of the breakout phase, Dr. Jack would wait until he felt they were fully on board. Then he'd gently ask, "So, what would you like to do about this?"

Often, they'd say, "I'd like to get this fixed!" and then we'd transition into the close. They understood the problem, they knew the solution and now it just came down to money.

And that's where I came in. I was the new closer. While I didn't leap with joy over my new role, I will say I didn't hate it as much anymore. I guess that's progress. Isn't it?

The first time Dr. Jack stood up to leave, my heart leapt into my throat. He said, "Miss Helen, I'm going to leave you in the capable hands of Dr. Bill, who will go over the financials with you. Then we'll meet up again directly after, OK?"

I squelched my urge to follow Dr. Jack out the door and silently watched him close it. The click of the door closing suddenly sounded deafening. It seemed as if Dr. Jack had taken all the air out of the room with him.

Helen turned and looked at me expectantly. My mouth was as dry as cotton and I suddenly forgot everything I knew. Looking down at the paperwork in front of me, I shuffled through it.

"Uh, um," I stuttered, picking up the financial form. It laid out the various payment choices. I must have picked it up and put it down several times. I stumbled quickly through a vague explanation about the therapies and adjustments. I'd rehearsed this a few times, but bungled it horribly face-to-face with this prospect. My words made little sense and I knew I was probably just confusing poor Helen.

How am I going to ask her for money?

My forehead beaded with sweat as my throat developed a golf ball-sized lump that no amount of swallowing could handle. I crossed and uncrossed my legs for the third time and said, "What I mean to say is..."

She kind of cocked her head to the side, her graying curly hair bouncing slightly. "You're kind of new at this, aren't you?"

"Yeah," I said exhaling a gust of air.

"Let me make it easy for you. All I really care about knowing is the cost."

"Right," I said. "Right. Well, let's go over that."

She smiled slightly. "Just give me the bottom-line number. What do I need to pay?"

I looked over her records and sighed in relief when I saw that she had excellent insurance coverage. I felt a lot of the tension leave my body as I said, "Wow, it looks like your out of pocket is three hundred for the twenty-four-visit treatment plan. Your provider will cover the rest."

"I can do that!" she said, giving the table a little pat. "So, what do I get for that?"

Now that she'd agreed to pay, she was closed, albeit accidentally. Now, I could relax and just go over the entire plan with her in a coherent way. She was very kind and forgiving of my stumbling errors.

When she left that evening, Dr. Jack patted me on the back. "It will get easier. I promise."

"I sure hope it will," I said, wiping my brow.

"We'll practice it a bit more," he said, patting me on the back. "Then you can try again."

As I watched Dr. Jack retreat to his office, it suddenly dawned on me that he'd probably arranged for Helen to be my first prospect, because she was an easier close. I felt a surge of warmth for my understanding mentor.

TWELVE

It was painfully clear that I needed to practice my communication—a lot more. I wrote out some potential dialogue and repeated it over and over, in the shower, in the car, even in front of Jacob and Mom. I went over and over it until I knew it cold. I swore I'd never be so tongue tied again.

When I was confident I knew my stuff, I told Dr. Jack I was ready to try again. He offered to sit in with me and the patient and I readily accepted. Although the thought of having my mentor watch me was a bit nerve wracking, I knew it was the best way to improve.

I did my best to pretend he wasn't in the room and gave my pitch to the client and his wife. I had it down. I had rehearsed it well and could explain all the benefits of chiropractic to both of them. It was a sweet summary of everything we'd explained earlier that evening.

They asked two questions and I answered each one perfectly. I was especially proud of my delivery. When I got to the part about the money, I took a deep breath and explained how much it would all cost. They didn't have insurance, so they'd need to pay out of pocket.

Once I finished my delivery, the man and woman decided it was too expensive, thanked us and left. Since they were the last couple of the evening, Dr. Jack sat down with me.

"So," he said, scratching his head "how do you think *that* went?"

"Good," I said. "I mean, *I* did well."

His brow scrunched slightly. "How do you figure that?"

"I didn't flub it. My presentation was good."

"But they didn't sign up."

"No, no, they didn't," I said, "but they seemed interested in what I was saying."

"I'm curious, why do you think they were interested?"

"I don't know. They asked questions, I guess?"

"Hm," he said with a thoughtful look. "Didn't you feel like you were doing most of the talking?"

I nodded. "Sure, but that's the way to close."

"Really?" he asked, looking confused. "Why do you say that?"

"In order to get them to pay, you have to explain why."

"Is that working for you?"

My head was spinning. Why was he asking me all these questions? Then I thought about how the couple had walked out and realized something was off. "No, I guess not."

"No," he said. "Do you know what went wrong?"

I shook my head. "Not really."

He leaned in and gently said, "I'm afraid the whole pitch was all about you."

No, you're wrong! "But..." I started in an attempt to defend myself then I stopped. In a sudden burst of clarity, I realized he was spot on. I had done almost all of the talking. Somehow, in all the confusion, I'd forgotten to make it about them, the client.

Damn! Wouldn't I ever learn that lesson?

Dr. Jack waited until I looked back up at him. When my eyes met his he said, "The other thing I noticed was that you kept cutting them off."

"No, I didn't..." As the denial fell out of my mouth, three instances where I'd interrupted the prospect to explain something popped into view. I closed my eyes, hung my head sheepishly, and said quietly, "I was excited."

He patted my arm. "Sure, and that's great! You should be, but the whole thing is that you need to get *them* to talk. They need to get excited about the treatments."

"But I have to explain it, right?"

"Think about how we ran any of the other segments. Really look at it. We always consulted the prospect. In the breakout sessions, did I ever *tell* the client what was wrong with them?"

I thought back and realized Dr. Jack had lead them in the right direction with the lecture, but he'd never actually diagnosed them. Instead he confirmed *their* diagnosis. "But...don't I have to *sell* them?"

"Actually, if you do it right, they sell themselves. After all, we put a lot of time in on educating them and showing them their X-rays, right? In the last phase, they've got to put two and two together for themselves. It's got to make so much sense to them that they don't see any other option than what you're offering."

It was an "ah ha moment" that reverberated through my entire body. "And you do that by asking them questions!" I murmured.

"And?" he prompted.

I grinned. It was all coming together. "And listening."

"Exactly. It's got to be like, 'I would be stupid not to do this.' You ask the questions then *they* arrive at the conclusion *you* want them to reach—that this process is the *only* answer for them. It's the solution they've been waiting for."

"Wow, so in the end, it's their decision," I said. The clouds of confusion had dissolved and the sun was peeking out.

"And remember, we've given them all the information they can digest in the lecture and the breakout. They know what they need to know. Don't rehash it all. There's no need. You'll just lose them. It's your job to continue to build the momentum, keep it going, right up until they pay for the service and receive that first adjustment."

As I walked away, I knew I needed to hone my pitch way down to just a few sentences. I was glad I'd spent the time really learning the larger speech. It wasn't a waste of time, as I knew that would come in handy down the line, but for the close, I needed to keep quiet and let them speak.

Over the next week, I met with a number of patients, but closed very few who didn't have insurance. Out of those who were self paying, the ones I closed only signed up when I offered them a substantial discount.

Dr. Jack asked to sit in on a few interviews with me. I agreed, eager to improve. The next couple I tried to close were in their twenties. The man, Alfred, had injured his back badly on the job and desperately needed our help. Dr. Jack sat next to me, but remained silent.

"Alright," I said a little nervously, "so I listened to your conversation with Dr. Jack and am really excited that you're going to get started with your care. Are you ready to get started?"

Alfred and his wife nodded, so I gave my shortened pitch and went over all that we'd offer him. Our treatment plan covered not only twenty-four adjustments, but personalized therapies and exercises. I laid out the costs for all the treatments involved, which worked out to twenty-five hundred dollars.

Next, I whipped out the Health Investment Options Form, which offered two basic choices. He could pay upfront and get a ten percent discount or he could make three monthly payments.

"So, since you don't have insurance, the amount you'd need to pay is twenty-five hundred," I said.

Alfred and his wife fell quiet as they reviewed the form. As the clock in the room ticked off the seconds loudly, I felt more and more uneasy and antsy. This program was too expensive for them and I couldn't help but feel guilty. As Alfred and his wife remained silent, I fidgeted, glanced at Dr. Jack and said in a rush, "I know that's a lot of money. It's a high price."

I could feel Dr. Jack wince next to me.

Alfred looked like I'd just given him a Christmas present. "It sure is!"

"I'm sure we can work something out, Mr. Alfred," I said with a smile. I looked over at Dr. Jack, who shook his head slightly.

I could feel Dr. Jack's disapproval in the pit of my stomach, but I was confused. Here was a man who needed chiropractic more than most. Being an independent contractor, putting up dry wall was the only way he could support his family. Every day off the job meant ruin for his wife and child. My heart went out to him and the truth was, I would have adjusted him for free.

What was wrong with that?

THIRTEEN

I hesitated for a moment, knowing that Dr. Jack wasn't pleased about some aspect of the conversation, but I plowed on. Maybe I hadn't been clear. Maybe Dr. Jack didn't understand my plan, so I explained. "Dr. Jack, couldn't we allow Mr. Alfred to pay over twelve months and maybe reduce the price a little?"

Dr. Jack looked over at Alfred with a sympathetic look. "Could you excuse Dr. Bill and I for a moment?"

Alfred nodded his head and said, "No problem. Gosh, Dr. Jack, if you could find it in your heart to make an exception for me, I'd be obliged. I mean, my wife and I here really see how much we need your help and care. I just can't afford it. It's a of money, you know."

"Just give me a moment, Mr. Alfred," he said. "We'll be right back."

I stood up and followed, glancing back at Alfred and his wife, who appeared to be praying for a successful outcome. I gave him a reassuring nod and closed the door behind me. Dr. Jack took me into Dr. Lorenzo's office and closed the door.

"I know your heart's in the right place, but you can't do that," he began.

I cut him off. "Can't do what?" I didn't understand why any of this was a problem. The deal I'd proposed would still bring money into the clinic. It was just a reduced rate.

"You offered a discount," he said with a shake of his head. "That's just not good business."

"Why?"

"Well, for one thing, think of all the other people who are paying full price. What will they say when they find out?"

I opened my mouth to respond and realized that he was right. That was a problem. Would they all now demand the same treatment? "Oh," I said.

"Not only that," he said, "but you just devalued what we do here. You devalued yourself, me, and chiropractic in one fell swoop!"

I plopped down onto one of the cushioned chairs in the small office. "How did I do that?" I asked, feeling a lot less certain about my position than I had a few minutes ago.

He sat down next to me and leaned in. "Do *you* feel that we charge too much?"

I thought about it. "No," I said.

"Why?" he asked.

"Well, for one thing, you have an office to run," I said. "Overhead, salaries, and other things.

"That's true," he said. "Can you think of anything else?"

I looked around and saw Dr. Lorenzo's certificates on the wall.

He had a few. "We all went to school for six to eight years. That's worth something."

"Damn right it is!" Dr. Jack said, slapping his knee with his hand. "They're paying for our skill and expertise. We do what we can by law, but we can't give it away for free!"

I nodded. "So, now what? He's expecting a discount now."

Dr. Jack waved his hand. "I'll go in there and handle Alfred. I'll see if he can stretch the payments a little further so he can get the care he needs."

"I'm sorry," I said.

"Don't be. If you learn, it's OK." He got up and walked to the door. "I'll be back. I want to finish up with this couple then I want to continue this conversation."

I waited in the office, glancing at my watch every other minute. Thank goodness it didn't take long for Dr. Jack to return.

"How did it go?" I asked eagerly.

"He signed up," Dr. Jack said. "We extended his treatment payment and he was happy."

"Good," I said with a smile. I was glad that Alfred was going to get the treatment as he really needed to get back on his feet.

"It's interesting to note," he said, sitting down next to me, "Alfred kept saying it was a lot of money. He got that from you, you know. Verbatim, that's what you told him. You gave him the ammo to use against you."

I winced. "Guess I did. I won't make that mistake again."

"Good! So, now that we have some time, I wanted to go over another key point in closing. You made a mistake that I think every newbie makes. What do you do when you pitch the price to the client? Do you know?"

I shook my head. "I just try to convince them. That's closing."

"No," he said, "it's not."

"What do you mean?"

"When you give him the price, you should have already set him up so that he knows everything he needs to know."

I nodded. "Yeah, but..."

"But what? Either you have or you haven't. When you give the price, you need to be certain they have all the information to close. If they don't, don't get into the price. There's a saying with sales, you know."

"What is it?"

"The first person who talks loses."

"Huh?" I'd never heard that before. That was crazy!

Dr. Jack smiled patiently. "Think about it. What happened right after you mentioned the price to Alfred."

I shrugged. "I don't know. I waited a bit and he didn't seem to be going for it, so I..." I thought about it, running the conversation through again in my head. "I felt sorry for him. I wanted him to know that I understood."

"You did more than that. You started back peddling." When he saw I was about to object, he raised his hand. "No, it's natural. People want to fill a silence with something, anything or they feel uncomfortable. It's something you'll need to practice, but when you give the price, you must stop talking. Let the prospect be the first to say something."

"What if they don't say anything?"

"Wait."

I was baffled. "It sounds like we'll get caught up in some kind of bizarre staring contest."

Dr. Jack laughed. "It doesn't usually go that far. The other guy will say something."

"Because they feel uncomfortable?" I asked. It was starting to make sense.

"Exactly. And if they don't give a yes, then try sticking with asking him questions. The trick is to get him to come up with an answer that will help him reach the conclusion you want him to reach."

I processed his words, nodded and said, "I'll try that."

"And whatever you do, don't answer their questions for them," he said with a chuckle. "Don't cut them off. Give them time to figure it out."

I tried this technique over the next few weeks and learned to stop offering discounts. My closing ratio improved, but the numbers still weren't what I wanted them to be. Since Dr. Lorenzo was also training on closing, Dr. Jack called us both in for a heart to heart.

"OK," Dr. Jack said, looking at both of us. "What's the number one problem you two are running into."

Dr. Lorenzo and I looked at each other and kind of shrugged. "People just aren't signing up," I offered.

"But why? What are they saying?" Dr. Jack said.

"They almost all say they need to talk it over with their husband or wife," I said.

"Ah ha!" Dr. Jack cried.

"It's reasonable," Dr. Lorenzo said. "I mean, I get it."

Dr. Jack nodded. "Of course, it is. In fact, I'll go as far to say that if the spouse isn't there, it's unlikely they'll be able to make the decision. Bill, you're not married yet, but when you are, you'll see that your wife won't be too happy if you agree to plop down two grand on *anything* without consulting her first."

"I'm sorry, but I don't get that," I said. "Wouldn't they want their wife or husband to get care, to get better? I'd think they'd be all over that."

"They might be *if* they were there for your pitch. However, since they weren't present, they have no idea of the value of your service. Most likely, they're getting some watered down version their spouse gives them. In the end, all they hear is that it's going to cost a couple thousand dollars."

I thought about it. It was true, in those instances, the spouse never got to learn how to read an X-ray, nor did they get to see their spouse's film. No, all they really understood was the price tag. Without the understanding of what they'd be getting, who in their right mind would agree?

I nodded. "I guess that's probably true if you're buying a new car or a refrigerator or anything really."

Dr. Jack said, "Sure, with any sales, it's always smart to meet with both partners. Ever notice that insurance salesmen always come to the client's house to meet with the husband and wife. Why do you suppose they do that?"

"Because they want to answer the spouse's questions personally," Dr. Lorenzo supplied.

"Right. And he wants to be there to *hear* their objection himself."

"You know," I said with a sudden jolt, "it's possible that the spouse might need treatment, too."

"They usually do," he said with a nod. "And you're right, they're more likely to sign up if they are there through the whole process. Either way, we need them there."

I frowned. This was all unfair. I always asked people to bring their spouse. "What if you invite them to bring their spouse and they just don't? What am I supposed to do then?"

"Well," Dr. Jack said. "What do *you* think we should do?"

"Uh, I don't know. I can't force them."

"Why not?"

"Hm?"

"I'm saying, I think we should ask them to leave and come back another day, with their spouse. Or not come at all," said Dr. Jack.

"That's a bit harsh, don't you think?" Dr. Lorenzo said.

"No," he said with a shake of his head. "The numbers don't lie. Most patients that come in without their spouse for their report of findings never return. They don't sign."

"So, you want me to actually refuse a client?" I asked.

"You're not refusing anyone. You're just setting policy. Do it in a friendly way, but let's try sending them home if they show up alone."

So, the entire office started turning people away for their report of findings if they failed to bring their spouse. These prospects weren't happy about it, but we found that most people returned within the week with their loved one.

And the numbers improved.

CONFIDENCE

Dear Bianca,

As you grow into adulthood, you're bound to hear me talk about the principles of leadership, as that subject is near to my heart. There are so many lessons you will learn throughout your life, but for me, the most valuable was realizing I needed to stay true to my authentic self.

I will admit to you that I tend to want to please everyone. I want to be all things to all people. Through years of experience, I've learned that just doesn't work. However, I've discovered that when you stay true to your principles, you tend to raise the level of the people around you and the people you serve. The bottom line is, remember to always serve others in a way that aligns with your values and your purpose.

Before you lead others, you must lead yourself. You must be a leader of your own life. That means you are aware of who you are and keep what you stand for in the forefront of your mind. This will require inner strength and confidence.

For, if you are secure in your own values and hold true to your integrity, you'll naturally attract the attention of the best people. Believe me, they will notice and respond.

Love,

Dad

FOURTEEN

After a couple months, I had quite a few more patients, but still not near the range I wanted. One weekend, I went home to relax. It was nice to get a change in space once in a while, be home with people who weren't involved with work.

Sitting on the front porch, I twirled a bottle of water in my hand. I looked over at my brother and asked, "How are things going for you?"

He shook his head. "Don't ask."

I chuckled. "That bad?"

"It's just so hard. Home security's fine and all, but I'm just not into it."

"Then why not change things up?"

"And do what?" he scoffed. "I've been doing this long enough that I finally have some seniority with the company. If I change out, I'd need to learn all about something new."

"It all takes work, but why not put your energy into a field you're on fire about?"

"I don't know..."

"Oh, come on. Don't you want to make a change in the world? Somehow?" I prodded.

He thought for a moment. "Well, I suppose I'd like to help people like Mom be able to buy their own house. I mean, she's worked her butt off all these years and has nothing to show for it."

I nodded. "It kills me that she continues to pay rent to the landlord. It's a sweet deal for him, not so much for Mom."

Jacob sat up. "You know, if I got into real estate, I could find her a good place, something she could call her own!"

"Bingo!" I cried, feeling like I was channeling Dr. Jack Ramsey. "Yes! Do that."

"It would mean a lot of study, getting trained," he said, crumpling back into his seat. "I don't know..."

I shook my head. "Don't you dare give up on that idea. Let's see. What's the first step?"

"We'd need to figure out the licensing requirements."

"OK! Let's do that now."

We spent the evening studying up on all the Illinois state requirements for becoming a real estate agent. Jacob groaned when he read that it would require ninety hours of study.

"It's going to take work, bro. But look here," I said pointing at the screen, "you can study online. That makes things easier."

He nodded and signed up right then and there for a course. At that moment, I knew he'd be finally following a path that he'd enjoy long term. I wanted him to stop being one of those people who got stuck in a career path they hated. People worked most of their lives, doing things they really didn't like. That made me sad.

Watching Jacob's eyes light up felt good. The feeling was similar to the one I got when I helped someone heal through chiropractic. One day, I planned to help others find their inner entrepreneur, their passion in life.

The next morning, I got up early and stopped in to say *hello* to my old chiropractor, Dr. Tracy. He was happy to see me, but gave me a sideways look. "How are things going?" he asked, his voice laced with concern.

I shook my head, "It's OK."

"Come on, Bill, I've known you forever. Maybe I can help."

I sighed and sat down. "It's just that Dr. Jack has me closing now and I hate all the no's. Every time someone walks away, it's a failure. I really can't stand it."

"Well," he said. "the first piece of advice I can offer is to try not to bring home the frustration."

"Easier said than done," I grumbled.

"Yeah, I know, but you've got to compartmentalize."

"How?"

He sat down next to me. "Well, let's start with this. Are you giving it your all?"

I ran my hand through my hair. "I think so."

"'Cause if you're not, you'll have lingering regrets. You've got to focus on making yourself the best chiropractor you can be," he said.

I couldn't help rolling my eyes at him. "But I'm not a salesman."

He laughed. "Come on now, Bill. Anyone who runs their own business is in sales! You must know that by now."

I looked at him and nodded. When I really thought about it, I realized I didn't hate sales as much as I had. I just wasn't as good as I could be and that's probably what bothered me the most. I should be converting more prospects into patients. Suddenly, it dawned on me, I needed to study sales as its own subject. I'd trained to be a chiropractor, but school didn't prep me for selling.

"Do you have any books to recommend?" I asked, feeling energized again.

"Now you're talking!" he said. "Yes, I have a few in the office and can suggest a few you for you to pick up."

So, with that, I began studying the art of sales. I read everything I could get my hands on and really absorbed what the experts had to say. It was then that I realized I wasn't alone in my troubles. I was hitting something most people did: The dreaded, *I need to think about it.*

I'd grown to accept that response as an unfortunate fact of sales. It hit me that this was a huge mistake. There really shouldn't be any reason for someone to think anything over. After all, we'd painstakingly given them all the information they needed. After the second day we'd invested in them, it was safe to say that they were no longer new to chiropractic. So, why weren't more prospects converting into patients?

The books all said that time and money were the two big culprits. It's seemed true to me. But what could I do about those two factors?

I asked Dr. Jack for his thoughts and he asked, "Have you been researching your clients before you sit down with them?"

I shook my head. "What do you mean?"

"You've got to study their folder, before you talk to them. The reason they came in is always in there, because we always ask. People have a reason for getting adjustments."

"I just figured they came in because they were hurting. Pain always seems to be their motivation, right?"

He shook his head. "No, there's usually an underlining goal they have. Pain can be part of it, but they almost always want to achieve something. That's what you need to know before you can close them."

"Oh," I said. He was being polite, but I knew he'd told me that before. I just hadn't been listening. I didn't think it was important, but now I realized I'd failed to listen once again. I needed to really hear the patients and fully understand their issues.

I took the time to really study each patient folder and realized there was a lot of information in there that I'd been missing. For instance, some people had a concern on our office hours, because they got off work just as we were closing. Fortunately, Dr. Jack allowed some flexibility on our hours and permitted us to stay late if needed. I could use that to close the person.

As I read various books on sales and practiced better techniques, I started to put everything I could into each interview. I didn't leave anything behind and was no longer afraid of the prospect. I was blunt, but loving; caring, but not afraid to push for an answer. It dawned on me that no's weren't my enemy. Sure, they never felt good, but they felt a lot better than a maybe, which usually resulted in the person walking off without getting a care.

As I sat down with Mr. Henry and his wife, Pat, I showed them their financial options, laid out the bottom line and looked at them as they studied the form. The silence might have been deafening to me a few months ago, but now I patiently waited for them to speak.

"I don't know Dr. Bill. That's a bit pricey," Henry said.

I smiled at the man. "The good news is, we can break that up into three payments," I said tapping that section of the form. "Makes it easier for you."

"Still, it's expensive," he said.

"I appreciate what you're saying, Mr. Henry. But, am I right that you've been on medication for some time?"

He nodded sadly. "Two years, ever since the accident."

"And you want that to change, right?"

"Of course," he said, sounding sad. "But I can't afford this."

Now, a few months ago, I would have jumped to offer him a discount. I knew he wasn't a rich man and he didn't have insurance. I couldn't bear the thought of him leaving without a commitment, because I knew we could help him. The truth was that I was desperate to give him that first adjustment that night, because it would put him on the road to recovery.

However, I wasn't even tempted to devalue our service. What we offered was a lifesaving, life-giving opportunity. Really, for this man, no price tag was too high for what we could do for him.

I leaned into him, with love in my heart, which I knew I wore on my sleeve. "Henry, can you really afford *not* to sign today?"

He looked me in the eye. Again, I resisted the urge to say anything more. I held his gaze, not my breath, and remained confident and certain of what I was offering him. Finally, he broke away and turned to his wife, raising his right eyebrow slightly.

That was a communication. He hadn't spoken, but he'd said

something very powerful to his wife. I realized then and there, it didn't have to be verbal. I could see he was asking his wife to weigh in, so I turned to her and said, "Pat, don't you want to see Henry's pain go away? Don't you want to see him off those awful pain meds? How important is that to you?"

She looked at me, tears welling in her eyes. "It means everything to me, Dr. Bill. Everything."

I softened my voice and allowed her words, her emotion, to flow through me. "I know it does, Pat. I know it does. So, let's get him the treatment he needs."

They both fell silent for a moment. Then Henry looked up at me and said, "We really need to think about it. I can't make a decision like this right now."

There was no way I was going to let them leave this room without a decision. And that decision had to be an emphatic yes. I needed to give Henry his first adjustment that night. I knew we could turn his life around and it was *my* responsibility to make sure he didn't allow that opportunity to slip through his fingers.

There was a certain feeling of power and joy in that realization. I was responsible. I was the one in the driver's seat. Not Henry. And I knew he knew that, too. He was asking for my help, counting on me to close him. He wouldn't be there, in my office if he weren't relying on my ability to help him.

"I understand completely," I said. "I'm going to leave the room and give you all the time you need to think it over. You just let me know when you're ready. Mr. Henry, I'm confident that you and your lovely wife, Pat, will reach the right decision. And please, let me know if there is anything I can do to help. Anything at all!"

I walked out and closed my office door behind me. Henry and Pat were the last couple of the evening. Dr. Jack gave me a questioning look, but I just explained what was happening and he looked at me with respect. "They'll close," he said.

"I know," I said with a confident smile.

And they did. They were both very happy in the end. After a few visits, Henry was able to stop taking half of his medication. And after another ten visits, he was completely off the drugs. It took a while for him to be pain free, but we got him there and he became a new man.

Henry's testimonial is one I have used over and over to help other people make the right decision. He became our poster boy for what one could achieve when one took the reins back and allowed their body to heal.

FIFTEEN

After succeeding with Henry, I continued to secure many patients for Dr. Jack. He nicknamed me, "The Closer," which appealed to my competitive nature and growing self-confidence. However, it left me with a hollow feeling inside. It wasn't the role I dreamed of. No, it was a far cry from what I'd envisioned for myself. I wanted to save the world.

Bottom line, I wasn't happy. Now that I'd mastered closing and marketing, I found myself bored and grumpy. I wanted the opportunity to make a lot more money. I felt myself bristling anytime Dr. Jack asked something of me. Despite my best efforts to hide my emotions, I knew my unhappiness and frustration were palpable.

One day, Dr. Jack invited me to lunch. He said he wanted me to meet a couple friends, Dr. Tony and Dr. Henry, fellow chiropractors. Eager to get out of the office, I agreed. After exchanging pleasantries, we ordered drinks and Dr. Tony explained that he and Dr. Henry had purchased clinics around the Chicago area.

Listening intently, I learned that they had created a profitable system. They had set up doctors in viable clinics they'd purchased and given the doctors a chance to run the clinics with a potential to purchase.

As Dr. Tony continued to speak, I realized that this lunch was in fact an interview and they intended to offer a clinic to me. *My own clinic.* Their words became muffled as I digested this concept. The room began to spin as I realized this was exactly what I needed, exactly what I wanted. It was the chance I'd been looking for.

Oh man, this is crazy. Am I hearing this right?

Dr. Tony looked me in the eye and said, "So, are you interested?"

Feeling confused, I glanced over at Dr. Jack to be sure he was on board with his friend's idea. He gave me a slight smile and nod. I knew at that moment, that he had picked up on my not so subtle cues. *He knew I was unhappy.*

I turned back to Dr. Tony. "Absolutely!" I could always switch gears quickly.

That seemed to impress them. "Good!" Dr. Henry said.

He and Dr. Tony then proceeded to ask me a ton of questions about my past, where I was from, how I got where I was, how I felt about working with Dr. Jack and my long-term goals. I fired off answers as rapidly as they asked them, opening myself up like an unfiltered blog post. I explained all my struggles, including my sports injuries, giving them as complete a picture about me as I could.

"So, where do you see yourself in five years?" Dr. Henry asked.

"I'll be running a million-dollar clinic," I said without hesitation.

I'd given that question a lot of thought. "And within ten, I'll be running several clinics, grossing ten million."

"Sounds like you have it all worked out," Dr. Henry said with an admiring smile. "And after that?"

I leaned forward and looked him in the eye. "My lifelong goal is to continue to expand my businesses, but add coaching to the equation. I want to help other docs, along with various entrepreneurs. I want to help people achieve their dreams and become the leaders I know they can be. Basically, I want to help people become the best versions of themselves!"

Dr. Henry and Dr. Tony exchanged looks, nodding to each other. "In the ten years I've been doing this, I don't think I've heard a better answer," Dr. Tony said. "So, do you have any concerns about running your own clinic fresh out of college? You'll need to manage employees."

"None, whatsoever," I said. I knew I sounded cocky, but I have always believed in presenting myself honestly.

"Excellent!" Dr. Henry said.

He went on to describe their training program in detail. All aspects of the presentations, business and technical application were fully drilled into each applicant prior to being unleashed into the clinic. I'd be learning all the protocols and procedures, including those of the team members. I'd also get indoctrinated into the software all the clinics used, so we'd be in sync.

"It takes about three months to complete our rigorous program," he continued. "You'll be given a small salary during this time and will be able to continue to practice in our clinic while you train."

I nodded. "What if I worked hard, passed all the tests, met all the standards? Could I graduate early and get into my practice?"

"Certainly!" Dr. Henry said. "It's never happened to date, but I can't see why you couldn't get it done in two." He glanced over at Dr. Tony, who nodded his greying head approvingly.

"When can I start?"

"How's Monday at 7:00 a.m.?"

Again, I looked over at Dr. Jack, who had been silent during the entire interview. He smiled, nodded and said, "Don't worry, I have a few replacement candidates in mind. You've become a valuable team member, but I would never hold you back from this opportunity."

A familiar warmth flowed through me as I realized he was giving up a lot by letting me go. He'd been an incredible mentor and I'd always be grateful. "Thank you!"

Dr. Jack leaned in and said, "You know, it wasn't that long ago that Dr. Tony took me under his wing and helped me get my start. I know what it's like to chomp at the bit to get started. I realized I could either pay you more or let you go. It's a decision we all have to make with our young up-and-coming stars. Don't get me wrong, I'll miss you, but it's time for you to step up to this new challenge!"

I felt the prick of tears form in the back of my eyes. He was giving up a lot to hand me a once-in-a-lifetime opportunity. I took a moment to really acknowledge his kindness before I turned back to Dr. Tony and Dr. Henry. "I'll be there at 6:30 a.m."

They both laughed. "Good answer! We'd like to show you the clinic you'll be taking over on Saturday before we start. It's important you know what you're getting into. How's 2:00 p.m.?"

I nodded. "Perfect!"

When I left I didn't think of all the questions I should have asked. I knew nothing about the demographics, the problems, the team members or the host of other difficulties they'd hinted plagued the small clinic. No, I had stars in my eyes, which outshone everything. Even when we visited the small strip mall, which hosted another, larger chiropractic office, I still was undaunted.

When I stepped through the door to my clinic, I didn't care that it smelled musty, that the space was tiny, and didn't notice that it looked worn and old. This was *my* clinic. It was special or at least, it would be when I stepped in and took over.

There's a brilliance to being naïve sometimes. If one is willing to put oneself out there and work hard, anyone can make any vision, any dream, a reality. I have always believed that knowing too much and siding with the norm of the world can stunt one's ability to dig deep down and take the necessary steps toward success. One needs a little freedom to make the life-changing mistakes necessary to achieve greatness.

SIXTEEN

The training facility was forty minutes from the current room I rented. Not bad. However, it would take me a good two hours to get to my future clinic. A move was in my future. That meant I needed to hustle through training and be frugal with my food budget, so I could afford a new apartment. The challenge gave me additional incentive.

As promised, I arrived at the training facility bright and early the next Monday—a little before six. I wanted to take my time to get a feel for the space before the rest of the team arrived. The first floor seemed deserted, so I began to explore, looking for signs of life.

The bottom floor was laid out similarly to Dr. Jack's office, but much larger. The adjustment area was huge and there were several rooms for examinations and consultations. After exploring the space, I made my way up the stairs to the second floor. Opening the door at the top of the stairwell, I found a wide-open space. There was a conference table on one end, with a projection system. I guessed it was probably for internal meetings. Along the east and west wall were a series of corporate offices for the executive team.

As I walked down the east bank, I noticed most of the offices were empty, but my eye caught a glow coming from one on the end. Feeling like a moth, I was drawn to the light. Peeking my head in, I saw a man sitting behind a desk, hunched over some papers, appearing to dwarf his furniture. He wasn't fat or skinny, just big.

Sensing my presence, he looked up at me and smiled. "You must be Bill," he said, his voice reminding me of a professional announcer. He was obviously a man of authority. When he stood up, he towered over me, looking to be well over six feet tall. "I'm Dr. Greg London, the Chief Operating Officer, or the COO."

"Nice to meet you, sir," I said, coming forward to shake his hand.

"Dr. Henry mentioned you might show up early. He said you were a real go-getter."

I returned his warm smile and said, "I have some serious goals."

"I heard," he said with an approving nod. "Impressive."

"Thanks."

"OK, well, continue your self-guided tour. Dr. Sheryle, your trainer, will be here in twenty minutes or so. She's always early, too. Just not as early as you."

"Looking forward to meeting her and the others," I said, turning to leave. "Thanks for the opportunity."

"My door is always open," he said. "Come by any time you like. I'm here to help."

"Thanks!" I said. "I really appreciate it."

As I walked out the door, I was happy I'd come so early. How many opportunities are there in life to meet a top executive on your first day, and one-on-one to boot? I went back downstairs and checked out the literature, familiarizing myself with the layout of the first floor. As the minutes ticked by the space began to fill up with doctors and staff until it was crowded with people.

The training officially started at 7:30 a.m., when Dr. Sheryle gave us all an introductory speech. Since we all wore name tags, I could tell that most of the participants appeared to be CTs (Chiropractic Technicians) and CAs (Chiropractic Assistants). And some people were also there to train in marketing, but only a few were training to own their own clinics.

We were all given folders with clinic protocols and guidelines to learn. Judging by its weight, it was a hefty assignment. I grimaced looking at all the memorization I'd have to do. That wasn't my thing. I considered myself to be more of a people person than a book learner, but it needed to be done. Sighing, I took off to try to find an undisturbed corner in that big hall. The open space wasn't conducive to quiet study.

Opening the folder, I admired the organization. There were multiple guides for every step of our process, each procedure and protocol. In addition, there were detailed instructions on team building and a thorough explanation of the software we'd need to use. Fortunately, everything looked familiar, because Dr. Jack had followed this program precisely. At least it wasn't all new territory.

After a few minutes, a young guy with jet black hair and wire-rimmed glasses put a hand on a chair next to me. He wore khakis and a light blue button-down shirt. His name tag told me he was a fellow chiro. "I'm Adam," he said, extending his hand. "May I sit here?"

"Sure," I said with a smile, accepting his hand. "I'm Bill. Looks like there aren't a lot of us here. Mostly CAs and CTs."

He nodded as he took his seat. "Yeah, I noticed that. Guess we'll be all working together in this cavernous room."

Looking around I saw that he was right. The Chiropractic Technicians were to our left, while the Chiropractic Assistants were grouping to the far side of the room.

We sat next to each other silently, each reading over our material. Feeling antsy, I soon realized I had to start practicing saying the words out loud. Turning to Adam, I said, "Mind if I practice these on you?"

"Not at all," he said, looking relieved.

It suddenly dawned on me that we were starting at the same point, so we could help one another. "Hey, why don't we team up? I'll start, then you can try it on me."

"I...I don't know," he said, shaking his head slightly. "I need some work."

I laughed. "Me, too. Memorization isn't my thing."

"Oh, that's not my problem," he said, waving his hand dismissively. "I take to memorization like a Wookie to chess. The words are easy, but it always sounds so..." he searched for the words.

"Wooden? Fake? Unreal?" I supplied.

"Uh, yeah, thanks," he said with a slight grin. "It's always nice to have my weak points pointed out by a total stranger."

"No problem, that's what I'm here for," I quipped. "Hey, seriously, I can help you with that stuff and you can help me, too. The sooner we finish, the sooner we can get in our clinics."

"That would be great!" he said, looking relieved.

"It will be more fun, too," I said.

We slogged through the initial exam and report of findings sections a few times before my stomach began to rumble. I glanced at my watch and realized it was just after noon.

As we ate and chatted, I realized how different we both were from one another. He was a little introverted and unsure of himself, while I was the opposite. The guy was a self-proclaimed nerd, owning five chess sets and over two hundred Star Wars books. About the only thing we saw eye to eye on was helping people through chiropractic. And football. But even there, we rooted for different teams. He was a Patriots fan, while I was a huge cheese head, following the Green Bay Packers. His intellect was well-suited for learning and memorization, while I had the emotion and passion to sell the words.

When we returned to the second floor after lunch, I jumped up the flight of stairs two at a time, opened the door and was greeted with the deafening sound of dozens of loud voices. The room was filled with smaller groups of people drilling procedures and practicing protocols. I groaned. I was having enough trouble getting the words down, and now I couldn't hear myself think.

SEVENTEEN

Adam came up behind me, stared at the room and paled. "This isn't going to work."

I nodded. "Yeah. I know." I jogged across the room, picked up our two packs, then turned back and walked down the stairs.

"Where are you going?" he asked.

"I'm not sure, but I have an idea," I said. "Come on!"

He followed behind me slowly, glancing back at the room before quickening his pace to follow me. "What do you have in mind?"

I looked around the first floor, noticing that the doctor report room was empty. I looked right then left before trying the door. Finding it unlocked, I went in and turned on a light. "We need our own space," I said. "And look, there's even a white board in here. It's perfect!"

"Yeah, but do you think anyone will mind?" he whispered.

"Why should they?" I said, closing the door. "The room's not being used and if they need it they'll tell us and we can go back upstairs. Sometimes you have to create the right situation, you know? I don't know about you, but I like being able to hear myself think."

With the closed door he and I could get loud. Really loud. We learned quickly to critique each other as we learned the procedures and followed the guides. We began politely, but after a few hours we felt comfortable enough to call each other out for every little error. We both wanted to ace this training, so we agreed to be hard on each other. As the days progressed it was clear that he and I made an excellent partnership. And fortunately, no one seemed to need that office.

"Just to give you some heads up, I plan to finish this program early," I said over lunch on the fourth day.

"Yeah? How early?"

"Tomorrow," I said without cracking a smile.

He burst out laughing.

"Seriously though, I want to break a record here," I said. "I plan to blitz this program."

"Like two months?" he asked, looking excited. "I'd love that."

"Why not? But, actually, I'm thinking six weeks."

"Really?" he exclaimed. "That would be crazy."

We scarfed down the rest of our lunch and walked quickly back to our safe training haven. I felt sorry for the others on the second floor, but was glad we had a place to really get into practicing.

We got to know each other very well, sharing our personal stories. He lived with his girlfriend, Candace, and had a close relationship with his mom. I told him about how I'd planned to become a professional baseball player throughout high school until my injury, and how Dr. Simon had helped me. Within a few days, Adam had become a second brother to me.

We did our best to make training fun, too. One day, I picked up a roll of paper and began whacking paper balls. Every time I got a specific wording down, he'd ball it up and pitch it to me, so I could hit it out of the park. It served as the perfect reward for getting it right.

I helped Adam get the emotion into the words. I wouldn't give him a thumbs-up if I didn't feel it. My harshness would annoy him sometimes, because he didn't exactly have a feel for it in the beginning, but by the end of the first week, he knew when his delivery sucked and when it was good. He became his own toughest coach.

My biggest problem was flubbing lines or simply going blank. Once I got the words down, he'd pretend to be a patient, so that I could practice handling questions. He'd come up with the most outrageous scenarios. Although I'll admit I found this annoying in the beginning, because it felt like he wasn't allowing me to complete a thought. But then, I got used to it, and realized he was helping me prep for any situation. After all, you never know what a patient might say in the heat of the moment.

"So, what are your goals?" I asked him when he'd finished up a series of patient scenarios. "Do you have any?"

"Yeah," he said. "I want to make some dough. And you?"

"I have a lot of dreams...a lot!"

"Like what?"

"Well, for one, I've had my eye on a CLS 550 Mercedes for some time," I said, describing the car in detail to him. "But more than that, I want a family and to give them the life I've always envisioned."

He pulled up a photo of a BMW on his phone. "This is what I want."

I nodded politely. It was a nice car, but it occurred to me that his dreams just weren't as big as mine. That was fine. We weren't cookie cutter imprints of each other.

"My first goal involves doing well enough with the company, so that they allow me to buy my clinic," I said. "That would mean I'd be making mid six figures."

"But only a handful of docs have done that!" he said.

I grinned. "That's right. Why shoot for less?"

He shrugged and mumbled, "Because it's more realistic?"

"Oh, come on. We're talking about *dreaming* here. Dream big, I always say."

He nodded and appeared to consider my words. "Owning my own clinic, eh?"

I nodded back at him. "Yessir!"

We continued to work hard, arriving a full hour before the rest of the trainees and leaving late. One evening, Adam and I were working on a particularly challenging procedural system. I was having trouble getting the words to come out right and he was having trouble keeping his eyes open.

Suddenly, we heard the door open and we both jumped, having had our backs to the door. There stood the large frame of the COO.

"You boys are up late," his voice boomed.

My heart raced as I took to my feet. Adam stood up, too. "Yessir!" we both said in unison.

He looked around the office. "I see you've commandeered the doctor's report room."

"It's too noisy upstairs," I said, holding my breath. *Please don't ask us to leave.*

He nodded. "Five years ago, when I went through this training, I did the same thing. My guess is that you're shooting for clinic ownership fast."

"That's right, sir," I said. "Within the first year."

He whistled low. "That would be fast."

"Yessir."

He laughed. "I believe you'll make it."

He bid us good night and walked out, closing the door behind him. I glanced at my watch. It was 8:00 p.m. "Guess we should call it a night."

"Yeah," Adam said with a yawn. "I thought you'd never ask."

I laughed. "I can't waste time if I'm going to finish training in six weeks and reach clinic ownership the first year."

That woke Adam up. "You were serious about that? The first year?"

"That's the plan!" Lead by example. It's the best way.

COURAGE

Dear Bianca,

One of my favorite quotes of Marianne Williamson is: "Our deepest fear is not that we are inadequate. Our deepest fear is that we are powerful beyond measure."

We all have limitless potential. Please never forget that and never underestimate your ability to be, do and have whatever it is you desire.

That said, fear is going to be a player in your life, but you get to decide how it affects you. Never let the presence of fear stop you from creating a wonderfully strong vision for your life. Many people refuse to shoot for the stars, failing to set challenging goals and expectations for themselves. This can create a lot of shame and regret when they reflect on what could have been.

The truth is, to be happy, to live fully, we need to consistently push ourselves to grow and evolve. If we do otherwise, we are just merely existing, not truly living. I believe the main reason we are *here, that we are given this precious gift called life, is to contribute our unique talents and passions to the world.*

Having a vision, with clear goals, allows you to live each day on a specific life path. Remember, having a direction in life is liberating! It gives each day a purpose that you design. We can never know how everything will work out or what will happen for us in life, but if you stay focused on your vision, it will help bring clarity in moments of difficulty and struggle.

Every person must choose whether to see the world as scarce or abundant. In scarcity, people tend to think the world is against them. My prayer is that you see how beautiful and abundant the world truly is! After all, with that mindset, you will consistently build strength during times of struggle and you might just see challenges as opportunities to overcome and grow.

Always know the strength you have inside!

Love,

Dad

EIGHTEEN

Within a few days, Adam and I were ready to enter the clinic and try out a few of the procedures with the clients. With all the rigorous drilling we'd done, we both found the practical assignment much easier. Real patients didn't often ask the off-the-wall questions that we threw at each other, but when people went *off-script*, we were prepared.

After a few weeks, we'd hit a rhythm and were way ahead of the pack. New doctors were coming in, but no one else seemed to think outside the box enough to find their own quiet spot to work. That was a blessing, as I'm not sure we would have been able to continue the way we were going if others clamored for the private offices.

One day, about three weeks into training, Adam and I were taking a break on the second floor when the Chief Marketing Director for the area rushed into the room. I watched her enter in from the opposite side and move from one doctor to another. Someone pointed at us and she charged over.

Out of breath, she shoved her wire-rimmed glassed up her nose. "Are you Dr. Bill and Dr. Adam?"

We nodded. "Yes, ma'am," I said.

"I need your help," she said.

"What can we do?" I asked.

"We have various outreach talks scheduled and I had all of them covered, but Dr. Chad called in sick this morning. Now, I need to find someone last minute to give this afternoon's workshop. It's at a bank. Someone said you might be able to do it. You've been flying through the training from what I hear. So, could you?"

Without thinking I said, "Sure, we'll do it!"

She was so grateful that she hugged Dr. Adam and I together. "Thank you! Thank you! I owe you big time." She gave me a folder with the pages of notes we'd need. We only had about two hours to prepare.

"*We?*" Dr. Adam said, paling slightly as she left.

"Don't worry," I whispered to him. "Just tag along for support."

"It's just that I'm not really that great in front of groups."

I put a commiserating hand on his shoulder. "Just think—what would Hans Solo say?"

"Um, he'd say, 'What's in it for me?'"

I rolled my eyes. "Fine, then Luke Skywalker. What would *he* say?"

"He'd do it."

"Well then?"

"Of course, I'll come with you," he said. "Let's go drill it."

I looked over the notes and drilled speaking about the topic, workplace safety ergonomics. When I arrived at the bank building, my palms were sweating, but once I started talking, my shoulders relaxed and it became second nature. As I eased into the role, I looked each participant in the eye. I infused the lectures with stories to keep the material less dry. No one glanced at their watch for the entire thirty minutes. They all seemed engaged.

Adam jumped in to answer a few of the questions the participants had. People responded well to him, too. In the end, the two of us signed up half the group for new patient appointments at the clinic.

On the way home, Adam was energized. "Checkmate, brother!"

I laughed. "We only got half. But yeah, that was a home run."

When we arrived back at the office, we were treated like conquering heroes. The marketing director was beside herself with our success and asked if we might be willing to do a few more lectures.

"Sure," I said. "We'd love to." It was good training.

At the end of the day, after everyone else had left, I gathered my belongings together and headed home. Motivated by my progress, I'd made the plunge and given a thirty-day notice to my landlord. The two-hour commute wasn't realistic. I didn't want to waste my life in rush hour traffic. The previous weekend, I'd signed a lease for a small studio near the clinic I'd be running. It was perfect, but twice the cost and I needed to come up with the first and last month, as well as the deposit, by the end of the week!

As it was, I'd been receiving a small salary during training, but that barely covered my necessities. I wasn't sure how to come up with the cash I'd need. Preparing for the inevitable doubling of expenses, I had been pinching pennies. My stomach churned as I opened the refrigerator and grabbed a chicken breast. Chicken and rice. I was so bored with it, but that was all I could afford.

That night I kept waking up, worried about my lack of funds. The only thing I could do was work harder, faster. But how could I do that on no sleep? Frustrated beyond belief, I couldn't get my mind to stop racing.

The next morning, I dragged myself into the office and managed to keep up with Adam. It took me twice as long to get through the drilling. If he noticed, he didn't comment on it. The next night I fell into bed exhausted, but still I couldn't sleep.

Finally, the next morning, unable to stay in bed any longer, I headed to the office early. The sun had yet to make an appearance, but I had to try to do something. Lingering in my apartment wasn't helping. The main floor was dark, so I stumped up the stairs to the second floor. Without thinking, I shuffled over to the only light on, the last door on the left, Dr. Greg's haven.

Seeming to sense my presence, he looked up and gave me a huge smile. When he noticed my bleary eyes and registered my distress he jumped up in alarm. He pulled out a chair and said, "What's wrong?"

I laughed and shook my head. "Do I look that bad?" I sat in the proffered chair and sagged.

He sat back in his chair and leaned in. "What's going on, Bill?"

I groaned. I shouldn't have come. What was I thinking interrupting his morning? I had no idea what to say, but I needed help and just found myself there. I trusted Dr. Greg. We'd shared a few heart-to-heart conversations over the past few weeks. He was a good listener.

I took a ragged breath in and said, "I can't sleep." I couldn't tell him all about my financial problems. I couldn't be that vulnerable and tell him how desperate I was.

He frowned and said, "Uh, huh," encouraging me to continue.

I shifted uncomfortably in my seat not knowing what to tell him. Obviously, he needed more of an explanation. The last thing I ever intended to share was that I didn't have the money I needed to keep up. However, under his careful scrutiny, I blurted out, "I'm running out of money."

I sighed heavily and dropped my head in my hands. If only I hadn't been so exhausted and frustrated, I could have come up with a better reply. All I could muster at that moment was complete honesty. "I'm sorry, I didn't mean..."

Dr. Greg put up his hand and nodded. "We don't pay you much in the beginning. I know that. Do you have any credit cards?"

I shook my head. "No, sir."

He studied me carefully. "How about your parents? Can they help?"

Again, I shook my head. "Sir, my mother works three jobs and still rents her place. She does everything she can and I'm proud of her, but I can't go to her for money. One day *I* plan to provide for *her*."

He silently nodded while walking back to his chair. Reaching into a drawer, he pulled out a checkbook, opened it and started writing. My heart raced as I watched his hand move. *Could he really be doing what I think he's doing?*

I had serious misgivings about taking money from *anyone*. But to accept a check from this man, someone I respected as much as I did, that was the last thing I wanted to do. He was the COO of this huge enterprise. I didn't want him to view me as some charity case. And what if I couldn't pay him back? Chills shot up my spine. That would be unthinkable.

Not sure what to do or say, I stared mutely at him as he ripped the check carefully from the checkbook and handed it to me.

I shook my head back and forth. "I can't." As I continued to stare at the check, I became tempted to reach out my hand to accept it. That little slip of paper was a life line, a chance for me to stop worrying about money and start focusing on what lay ahead.

"From what I gather, you don't really have a choice, do you?" he said, his voice soft.

My eyes flickered up from the check. "I have to come up with first, last and the deposit on a new studio."

He gave me a gentle smile. "So, if you don't take this, what will you do?"

I stared at him blankly. I didn't have a plan. I closed my eyes, overwhelmed with it all. One option was to keep my current apartment and make the two-hour commute each day, but even as the thought flickered through my mind, I knew it wasn't realistic, not in the long term. It would eat up all my time, time I needed to make this clinic a success. That was going to be tough and if I was going to do well enough to be able to purchase the clinic within the first year, I'd need to pour every waking minute into the project. I couldn't afford to spend four hours each day driving. Plus, the gas prices were soaring again.

Dr. Greg cleared his throat and I opened my eyes to look at him. "It's an investment," he said intently. "I believe in you, Bill. I want to give you every chance to succeed. Besides, if you do as well as I know you will, you'll be making this company a small fortune!"

Suddenly, I felt better. Grinning, I nodded. He was right, I would. I slowly, tentatively, reached out a hand. It trembled slightly as I accepted his check. Odd how that small slip of paper held the solutions to my current problems. "This is unbelievably generous of you," I whispered, feeling a rush of affinity. "However, I'll only accept it as a loan, not a gift."

He shrugged. "As you wish. It's not necessary, but I'll leave that up to you."

"I insist," I said with conviction, standing up. A burst of adrenaline spread through me as I realized I no longer had this barrier stopping me from accomplishing all my goals. "Thank you!"

He grinned. "Go on. Get out of here. I have work to do."

I smiled back. "Me, too."

NINETEEN

When Adam arrived, I greeted him with a new burst of energy. However, because my body was exhausted, I began waning mid-afternoon. When I fell asleep reading material in my chair, Adam pulled me up and pushed me out the front door. "Go get some rest," he said. "I'll see you tomorrow morning."

I considered protesting, but was too tired to argue. He was right —I was a mess. "Thank you, my friend," I whispered.

The next day I came in ready to conquer the world. I was determined to whip through all the training protocols in record time and help Adam navigate his way through the delivery. Anytime I wasn't drilling procedures with Adam in a room, I was watching the way the clinic worked, observing how the patients flowed through the procedures and how the doctors performed the therapies and adjustments. Getting the visuals made the words come alive. When I was ready, Adam and I began testing out our knowledge with patients, learning the procedures until we had them down cold.

I finished the training in less than five weeks, happy that I'd beaten the goal I'd set for myself. Adam finished soon after. He was motivated to finish, eager to start in his own clinic. And he seemed to have his eye on being a clinic owner after all our discussions.

As I gathered my things to leave, Dr. Greg came over and put his hand on my shoulder. "I'm proud of you. You know you smashed the previous record of seven and a half weeks!"

"It's a habit of mine," I said with a cocky grin. I put down all my books and papers and gave him a hug. "Seriously though, thanks for making this all possible."

"It was all *you*," he said. "Don't forget that."

I pulled back and admired how he was willing to give me the praise. He had every right to claim credit for my success. He had given me a lifeline, when I'd needed it the most. Yet, he was content to hang back in the shadows and applaud my efforts. I hoped I'd be the same one day.

"Are you nervous?" he asked.

"No, not nervous, just excited. Thanks to you, and this clinic, I'm ready."

Since I didn't have too many possessions, I knew it wouldn't take me long to move. I was relieved to have the weekend to settle. Jacob brought over a dozen good boxes and helped me put everything I owned into them, while I figured out what I could toss.

"Safe Home has these boxes just laying around," he said. "They were fine with my taking them off their hands."

"Still working in home security?" I asked. "How's your real estate course going?"

"It's going," he muttered.

"Having trouble?"

He shrugged. "It's just a lot on top of the overtime."

"I get that," I said. "But sometimes you just have to buckle down and get it done."

He upended my silverware drawer into a box with a loud clatter of noise. "It's too hard," he whined.

After having completed my training in half the expected time, I curbed my impulse to snap at him. He had no idea what tough study was! I sighed. Yelling at him wouldn't help the situation. Jacob never liked study, even when it was required work. This was optional, so it didn't surprise me that he was dragging his feet.

"It would be easier to just skip it," I said, thoughtfully. "But then you'd probably be working in home security for the next ten years."

He plopped down on a nearby chair then looked at me with a pained expression. "I don't want that."

Good! I was relieved that he wanted more from life. "Look, it's all about targets. When would you like to complete the course?"

"Tomorrow," he said.

That's my brother! "Well, OK, that might be a tad difficult, what with the whole pesky twenty-four hours in a day rule."

He nodded. "OK, realistically, I still have sixty hours of study left."

"Hey, that means you're a third done," I said. "That's not bad." I realized I'd come along way. Instead of berating him, I was encouraging his progress. *Where did I get that from?* Dr. Greg's face appeared before me as an answer. The gentle giant had rubbed off on me.

"Yeah, I guess," he said with a nod.

"So, what are you going to get done this week?"

He shrugged and slumped. "I dunno."

"Hey, don't do that. Don't give up."

"I'm not."

"Come on," I said with a smile. "Let's set a goal."

"I don't want to say anything, because then you'll get after me to do it." He looked up at me with a pained expression.

I laughed loudly. "Yeah, bro, that's the idea. You, like everyone, needs a little accountability."

He looked at me warily. "OK, I'll try to get three chapters done online this week."

I nodded, then thought of Adam. Channeling him, I said in my best Yoda voice, "Do or do not. There is no try."

He gave me a weary look. "When did you become a Star Wars geek?"

"That would be Adam's influence," I said.

"Ah," he said, nodding in understanding. "I can see that. He's a cool guy."

"So then, we're agreed? Three chapters," I said.

He nodded. "OK."

I made a mental note to check up on him mid-week to check his progress. Then, once he finished those three chapters, we'd set a new target. It was the only way we'd get him through this training and onto the career he wanted.

I feel I've found my calling! Helping others accomplish their goals and be happy with their occupations was a fundamental part of my life's purpose.

When Jacob left later that night, it didn't take long to unpack the rest of the stuff and make the new studio feel like home. I sat back in my recliner and closed my eyes, picturing the new clinic. Tomorrow would be the start of my new life.

TWENTY

Walking into the clinic the next morning was surreal. I was the first one there and realized I didn't really know much about my Chiropractic Assistant. The company had hired her to help keep things running until I could take over. I imagined what she'd look like sitting behind the front desk to the right and smiled.

Dr. Greg had explained that there was a chiropractor who'd been holding down the fort for me, coming in part time. I'd chatted briefly with him on the phone and had agreed to meet him bright and early. I wanted to get there before him, so that I could take stock of the office.

In the clear light of day, knowing this clinic was my responsibility, I began taking inventory of all the many problems. The walls needed a fresh coat of paint, and the rugs were in sore need of shampooing. Heck, even a vacuum cleaner would help. I walked down the corridor to the back and opened a small closet on the right, hoping to find one. Inside was an antiquated carpet sweeper.

Pulling it out, I heard the front door open. I walked back and was greeted by a woman with long blond hair, who appeared to be in her late twenties. She wore the traditional light blue scrubs.

"You must be the new doctor," she said, glancing at the sweeper in my hand. "I'm Valerie, your C.A."

I smiled and said, "Yes, I'm Dr. Bill. Nice to meet you!"

We shook hands before she went to sit behind her desk and turn on the computer. I was surprised that she hadn't taken the sweeper off my hands, but shrugged. I continued to sweep as much of the stray particles off the floor as I could, but it didn't make a huge difference. The floor still looked pretty horrible. The moment I could afford it, I was determined that we'd get new carpeting.

The chiropractor came in a few minutes later. He was so tall, I found myself craning my head up to look at him. "Sorry, I'm late," he said with a smile. "There was quite a bit of traffic."

"No problem," I replied, extending my hand. "You must be Dr. Tim!"

He eagerly grasped my hand in his. "That's right. And you must be the newly minted doctor, the one who's been breaking all kinds of records."

I felt my cheeks heat up a bit. "Thanks! Hey, do you have time to show me around?"

"Of course!" he said. "There's not much to see. And the good news is, you don't have a patient scheduled until one. That will give you time to familiarize yourself with things."

I nodded. "How many patients to do you see each week?"

Tim shrugged. "Not as many as I'd like, to be honest. Maybe

sixty or so? But I expect you'll turn that all around! This clinic's been part time for me."

"Hey, sixty isn't bad!" I said. "It could be a lot worse. So, I'm guessing that you have another clinic somewhere else?"

He nodded. "About an hour away. It's been tough splitting my time."

I gave a low whistle. "That's quite a commute!"

He shrugged. "Someone had to pick up the slack after the previous chiropractor moved to California. I didn't want to see the clinic close."

"Thank you for doing that!" I was grateful that Tim had kept this clinic going so well. "I'm looking forward to learning all about this place."

He grinned broadly. "That's why I'm here!"

He showed me around the office, which I gauged to be a little under twelve hundred square feet. Along the right wall, was an exam room and a room designated for X-rays, then on the left was a second exam room. Next to it was a tiny doctor report room.

"Where's my office?" I asked, looking around.

"Follow me," he said, gesturing down the hall.

I followed him straight back and discovered my office was right across from the closet where I found the sweeper. The room was about the size of a walk-in closet and doubled as the patient file room. It had a sliding glass door, which was in sore need of greasing.

As I took all the details of the office in, I mentally moved furniture around, creating better flow lines. After Tim finished the ten-minute tour, he said, "Well that's pretty much it. Maybe we can go over a few patient files."

"That would be great," I said. I hadn't realized that I'd been holding my breath until I exhaled. "That would help make the transition smoother."

"Exactly," he said guiding me back to my office. "I really care about every patient that comes through this door. It will be hard to say good-bye."

It took the better part of two hours, but by the time we were done, I felt more acquainted with my new patients. Tim shared little stories, along with their treatment successes.

"I've got to run now, but if you need me for any reason," he said, "any reason at all, I'll swing by to help."

I nodded. "Thank you. I really appreciate it!"

"My pleasure," he said and walked out the door.

I turned to look at Valerie, who was hunched over her computer. I glanced over her shoulder and saw that she had the software down and appeared to have everything well organized.

"Can I help you?" she asked. I wasn't sure if I was imagining it, but she seemed annoyed that I was there, watching her.

I frowned but kept my voice pleasant. "I was just admiring your work."

"Thanks," she grumbled, turning back. After a few minutes her eyes flicked back to see if I was still there.

Sighing, I threw up my hands and walked outside. I strolled around the little strip mall, noticing the neighborhood was a little impoverished. There were a half-dozen small businesses, including another chiropractic office. Peeking in, I grimaced. They were much larger than my clinic, with two doctors inside.

Sighing, I walked back. I certainly had my work cut out for me. Symbolically rolling up my sleeves, I began to plan ways to get new patients in. Fortunately, between Dr. Jack Ramsey and all the training I'd just received, I felt prepared.

TWENTY-ONE

I got on the phone and scheduled a few talks around town. This was *my* community now and I needed to get involved—find a way to reach people. By the time my one o'clock patient, Gloria, arrived I was eager to meet her.

I hung back and watched to see how Valerie would greet Gloria. Instead of giving a cheerful hello, my CA barely acknowledged the patient as she checked herself in with a swipe card. The middle-aged Hispanic woman, my first-ever patient, didn't seem upset as she put away her keys and started to stretch.

I waited to see if Valerie would come and get me to introduce me to her, but as usual she was entrenched in her computer work. Undaunted, I approached Gloria with a "Hello, I'm Dr. Bill." She broke into a genuine grin. It seemed to me that she was relieved by my friendly enthusiasm.

I took her back to the exam room and conversed with her a bit before her adjustment. Afterwards, she gave me a little hug and let me know that she felt better before she left. As I watched her leave, I noticed that Valerie didn't lift her head from her work.

Puzzled, I walked back over to her and stood there for a moment. Finally, when the minutes ticked by, I realized she didn't even know I was there, so I said, "Valerie?"

She flinched, then looked up at me. "Yeah?"

"You're my CA, right?"

"That's right."

I sighed. Well, at least we agreed on that. "OK, good. The thing is that I need you to help me with the patients. A CA isn't just all about the administrative stuff. You need to greet patients when they come in and give them a kind good-bye when they leave."

She sighed. "OK."

"It's important that they see a friendly face when they come in. We have no idea what's happening in their lives, what they might be going through. At least we can be a safe place for them to relax," I said.

She nodded. "I can do that."

"Good!" I said, sighing in relief. My shoulders relaxed and I realized just how tense I'd been. "That's great. Thank you!"

"Sure thing," she said. "Anything else?"

"Yeah, what's my line up for the week?"

She opened up the scheduling program and showed me the patients I had that week. The gaps were apparent, and I grimaced.

"Looks like I have work to do," I said more to myself than her.

Over the next few weeks, I threw myself into outreach programs, doing my best to bring in new patients. Back at the clinic, Valerie was trying to be more personable. The problem was that her basic personality was at odds with the demands of the job. Not wanting to be an overbearing boss, I just gave her slight direction then did my best to cover her shortness with more friendliness of my own.

As the number of patients coming through the door increased, I realized I'd need a Chiropractic Technician to help me throughout the day. It was too difficult to help people with their therapies, do the exams, on top of handling the adjustments. I was in sore need of help.

I interviewed several candidates, talking to them extensively about what I wanted. Looking over their resumes, I chose Robin Gilmore, a young girl who seemed serious about the work. Her ambitions were centered around making good money, which seemed correct to me. After all, since I had my heart set on becoming a clinic owner, why shouldn't she want monetary success?

The only negative thing was that she complained about her previous clinic. According to her, the patients were all problematic and the chiropractor was frustrated with them, and her, most of the time. However, she looked great on paper, so I hired her.

Having a C.A. and C.T. in place I could devote more time to expanding the practice. The first month was slow and I only secured five new patients. The second month was more promising with fifteen new signups.

One day, Dr. Greg gave me a surprise visit, offering to buy me lunch. I eagerly accepted, wanting to pick his brain for ways to improve the clinic faster. At the rate things were going, it would take years to get to a point where I could actually afford to buy the clinic.

"Looks like things are picking up," he said.

I nodded. "Just not fast enough."

"Well, what have you been doing?"

I thought about his question for a minute. "For me it's always been about getting through my fears so I can put myself out there to meet new potential patients. I've been focused on connecting my message to the prospect's needs and values. Building good relationships with local businesses is also key. However, that is always nerve-wracking. I still don't enjoy getting rejected when it happens, but the community has been pretty receptive overall."

"So, you're pretty laser-focused on that," Dr. Greg said with a smile. "How's your team shaping up?"

"Uh..." I said, feeling the room spin slightly.

"You hired a new C.T. last month. How's she working out for you?"

I shook my head. "Not great."

"Why?" he asked with concern. "What's wrong?"

"She's cold," I said with a frustrated sigh. "And she's kind of flakey, calling in sick at least once a week."

He nodded. "Tell me about her interview."

"Oh, she had a great resume!"

"Yeah? What else did you notice?"

I thought about it and said, "Well, Robin seemed pretty fixated on money. She mentioned it a few times."

"And what did you think about that?"

"I think that's fine. I figured that would mean she'd do a good job."

"Hm," Dr. Greg said, frowning slightly. "How so?"

"I figured that meant she'd be hungry. Like me."

He nodded. "While it's true that you're hungry for success, your heart is also in the right place. Honestly, it's a huge red flag if an applicant talks too much about money. You want someone who is there to help people. Especially your C.T.!"

Looking over it, he was spot on. Robin didn't really seem to care about her work. "I keep trying to get her to learn a little about each patient, but she doesn't seem to care."

"Anything else in the interview?"

"She was ragging on her previous clinic," I said with a sigh. "I knew that wasn't good."

Dr. Greg shook his head. "That's always a bad sign."

"Yeah, but I really wanted to overlook it."

"It's all a learning process. And your C.A.? How's she working out?" Greg asked.

"She was there before I came," I said with a shrug.

"I know, but how is she fitting into your clinic?"

I shook my head. "She doesn't seem to like people much."

Greg laughed. "Well, that's a problem!"

"Yes, it is," I said with a smile. "I'm seeing that I need to let them both go."

"Good! You can't just hire to hire. Always hire the best person for the right position. That way they can shine! The process should take time. Don't rush it."

I nodded. I needed to have a stellar team if I were going to hit my difficult targets. There was no way I could do this on my own. The C.A. and C.T. weren't employees in my book—they should be my extended family. And neither Valerie nor Robin fit the bill.

When I returned to the clinic, I had a heart-to-heart with both women. I really looked for good reasons to give each a second chance, but the truth was that they needed to go. Fortunately, after our discussion, it was a mutual decision and Valerie and Robin agreed to stay on as I began interviewing other candidates. I could spend the time finding the right team members.

TRIBE

Dear Bianca,

Develop your tribe with great intention, for they will be a reflection of you.

Simply put, surround yourself with people that have the same values as you do.

Take that a step further, and also gather around people that can support you in your weaknesses.

The members of your tribe might change as you get older. After all, you're bound to grow out of certain relationships and expand into others. It's all part of your personal development.

Don't simply spend your time with amazing peers. Instead, strive to find the giants of your profession and do everything you can to stand on their shoulders. Reach out to mentors, people around you who are succeeding in your community and seek their advice and guidance. Also, invest in yourself by traveling to conferences and *seminars to hear the greats speak whenever you can. This education will inspire you in ways you can't ever quite predict.*

Love,

Dad

TWENTY-TWO

Over the next two weeks, I took off some time from community outreach and focused on interviewing a few dozen people for the position of C.A. and C.T. Through that process I learned a lot. Greg's advice helped tremendously, and I found a few books in the library to help me as well.

Bottom line, I needed to ask difficult questions during the interview process. In addition, it was smart to test the candidates to be sure they'd be a good fit in the long term. With open-ended questions designed to encourage dialogue, I allowed them an opportunity to complain about their former employers. Having gone through what I did with Robin, I diligently dismissed any applicant who had any sort of critical remark. I completely focused on people who saw the world with an optimistic lens. I also did everything I could to encourage them to open up about their passions in life.

When Lewis strolled into my office, looking sharp with a suit and tie, I was immediately interested in him as my C.T. He wore a genuine smile and looked me in the eye as he spoke and listened. He was confident, but respectful. Lewis also exuded health, which was important for someone working in a wellness clinic.

As we talked, I immediately liked him, but resisted the urge to hire him on the spot. I continued to interview several other people, but noticed I was always comparing them to Lewis, finding them lacking in various ways. That's when I realized I had my new C.T.! I valued his caring nature and ambitious confidence.

Brene was my next hire. She was bubbly and a genuinely loving person. She gave me a hug after the interview, which made me smile. I wondered if she hugged everyone she met. I needed a mama bear to organize my inherent disorder, but I also wanted someone who felt real affection for our patients. She was perfect.

Between Lewis and Brene, I knew the clinic would expand quickly. They were both hard working people. I went back to focusing on outreach and the business side of things. It was a relief to be able to leave a lot of the background and administrative things to my two new team members.

On the weekends, I would meet with financial advisors and business minded people, learning everything I could from them. It didn't take long before new patients were flooding the small office. They continued to pour in and my numbers increased dramatically month by month. I'd talk to every group of new patients with assertive honesty.

After six months we reached over two hundred patient visits per week. Ownership was within reach. I could taste it. I saw my goals for financial freedom in sight and was in full throttle all the way.

Money was starting to pour in and I kept my head down and focused on bringing in new patients.

Unfortunately, over the next few months the numbers plateaued, then started to slip down. I was losing control and felt helpless to correct it. We were hemorrhaging patients as steadily as we'd been growing the months before, and I knew it had nothing to do with me. I was on *fire*.

So, it had to be by team. Frustration bubbled within me as I felt betrayed.

One day, when the lunchtime rush left, I turned to find an empty office. "How is this possible?" I said, my anger bubbling over. "This clinic shouldn't be empty at twelve thirty in the afternoon!"

Lewis looked at me with wide eyes. "I...I don't know."

"Brene?" my voice boomed out, reaching her in the other room. "What's going on?"

She rushed over to me and said softly, "We had a few cancellations."

"Really?" I asked, barking out a sarcastic laugh. "And you didn't think to tell me about that? That's a *problem*, don't you think? You're supposed to warn me before we hit rock bottom like this. That's your *job*, isn't it?"

She stared at me for a moment then nodded. "Of course it is, Bill. Why don't we sit down and go over it?"

I looked at her and frowned. "I don't have time to sit and *chat*, Brene."

"Yes, you do." Brene looking me in the eye with a no-nonsense expression, refusing to back down.

I curbed my impulse to continue to shoot venom at her and

followed her to my office. She pulled out a chair and indicated that I should sit. I did, but folded my arms across my chest and glared at her.

"You've changed, Bill."

I wasn't expecting that. "Come again?" I bit out.

She sighed. "You're upset because you've lost a few patients. Right? Well, you need to look at what *you're* doing to cause that."

What was she talking about? "So, you're saying it's *my* fault?" I didn't like the direction of this little heart to heart with my C.A. "I'm doing exactly what I'm supposed to be doing. I'm working my butt off bringing in new signups. *I'm* not the problem."

"This is your clinic now, so your job isn't just bringing in new business. You must manage the existing patients," she paused for a moment to let that sink in before she added, "And lead your team as well."

"What are you talking about?" I said, throwing my hands in the air. "I lead you guys!"

"*Do* you?" she asked. "You've never laid out clear guidelines for Lewis or me. We're both winging it, doing the best we can for *you*."

I opened my mouth to reply but closed it again. It suddenly dawned on me that although I'd done extensive training, they hadn't. I never explained what I expected of them. Suddenly, I was impressed that they'd gotten as far as they had without any real help from me. Somehow, I'd stopped being the compassionate leader I knew I could be and turned into some dictator. When had that happened?

Lost in my own thoughts, in my own world, I felt Brene put a gentle hand on mine. "Everyone loves you, you know. They just need to be *led* by you."

I nodded, my head swirling with the reality check she was giving me. "I can do that."

"Good!"

"Hey, let me get Lewis in here," I said. I brought him in to my office, dragging a chair behind me, so he could sit, too.

"I need to apologize to both of you. I think I've been too focused on the business side of things. I forgot that people are what make any business successful. I need to make some changes."

I asked both Brene and Lewis to critique my leadership, encouraging them to speak their minds. It wasn't always easy, but honestly, I needed to hear their truths. Beyond that, I think it wasn't bad for them to see me that vulnerable. As they spoke, I realized how lucky I was to have them. They were the team that would get us to ownership level and beyond.

TWENTY-THREE

Over the next few days our team had more huddles and discussed each patient in detail, together. As I helped them better understand my purpose, I also rekindled my own true goals. These patients were never just numbers. They were individuals with stories and I had the privilege to help shape each one. After each huddle, I felt an instant relief, because I knew the patients we discussed would continue to return for their treatments.

Brene continued to be a treasure. She helped remind me that I should continue to do all the things that I had done prior to becoming a business machine. I needed to let patients know I cared. In the confusion, I'd stopped calling all my new patients after their initial visits. That had always gone a long way to helping people feel special. I also followed up with each patient we discussed in the huddle who needed extra attention. Some had personal matters they shared during treatment, but others just needed to hear that we were committed to their success. After all, our patients were part of our extended family.

When the clinic's numbers quickly bounced back, I vowed to always do the little things that set us apart. That philosophy really applied to *any* business. If you want to retain clients, you can't just do your job at a bare minimum level.

I continued to read books, learning everything I could about building an effective team. I also hired Leslie, who was a patient, as an extra Chiropractic Technician. She had a vibrant, spunky personality. We'd talk through her therapy and I learned that she was fresh out of college and really didn't love selling ads for a newspaper all day. She enjoyed the people she worked with, but couldn't take all the rejections that came with her deflating sales job.

Leslie was a teddy bear, who naturally talked to the other patients when she visited the clinic. She had come to me with serious neck and shoulder pain, causing severe migraines. They put her out for days. She fully committed to a rigorous program, and together, we helped her eliminate a once debilitating condition. As a result, she began talking to me about switching professions and becoming a chiropractor.

"I'm looking for a second C.T. here. Interested?" I asked her one day as she was stretching.

"Really, you mean it?" She gave me a huge smile and appeared to be holding her breath.

"Yes, really. I know you love it here and you're so good with people. You'd be perfect! And it would give you a lot of training if you're still considering becoming a chiropractor."

"Oh, my gosh!" she cried. "That would be wonderful! I can't think of a better job!"

When Leslie started at the clinic it was like having a super compassionate Energizer Bunny. She was amazing for the culture, as she was beyond loving to all the patients. She added a light and cheery mood to the clinic, naturally, and she got along well with the rest of the team.

I realized I was in the homestretch and would reach ownership within the next month. Dr. Greg visited more frequently to help me fine tune my team. I hired another two people and continued to grow and expand.

Tim and I ended up bonding over our mutual goal to hit the top levels in our clinics. One day he called me and asked if I might like to meet another successful chiropractor in the area. Dr. Selina was an African American woman in her late thirties, who was taking the chiropractic world by storm. Excited, I was grateful to connect with Tim and Selena as we could all benefit from trading notes.

It didn't take long for us to become the three amigos. We'd get together every Thursday for dinner and strategize. Then we'd call or email each other throughout the week with new ideas and plans. Dr. Selina was a wealth of knowledge and she was always willing to share her experience to help me improve.

Our Thursday get-togethers began growing as word got around. Somehow many of the ambitious chiropractors in the Chicago area had heard about our little meeting. Before I knew it, we had to book a private room at the restaurant to accommodate the crowd. I invited Adam, as he had recently plateaued and wanted to reengage in his original plan to be an owner.

I also continued to seek out and interview top leaders in the Chicago area. I soon spotted that the successful ones each had a trait in common, something that set them apart from the pack. They were humble. And through them, I learned that a great leader takes full responsibility for everything. When good things happen, one should praise one's team. And when things go wrong, one must shoulder all the burden and never blame anyone for the errors.

I'd been doing the opposite. Even after my talk with Brene, deep down, I took all the credit for our clinic's successes. It was bullheaded of me. When I really took that additional inner step of giving my team the lion's share of the glory, everything came together. It didn't take long before I could take the next step and officially earn the right to purchase my own clinic.

It had been only a year and a half and I was consistently treating three hundred and fifty patients a week. I celebrated my victory by purchasing a black CLS 550 Mercedes, just like the one I'd always envisioned. While I could have afforded it earlier, I felt it important to wait until I'd hit the status before splurging. It was more meaningful that way. As I drove away from the dealership, I realized I needed a new goal. I'd been so focused on this one, if I wasn't careful, I'd get stuck and never continue to rise higher.

It was as if my new car had a mind of its own. I headed south on 57, toward Decatur. Although I hadn't lived there in a few years, it would always be home to me. And no success was worth anything if I wasn't sharing it with my family.

As I pulled up, Mom came out on the porch with a dish rag on her shoulder. She beamed at me as I parked the car then hurried forward to greet me.

"What are you doing home?" she cried, as she squeezed me tight. "And what are you doing in that shiny black thing?"

I grinned. "It's the one I've been talking about for years."

She feigned disinterest. "Really? I must not have been listening too carefully."

I chuckled. "That doesn't sound like you."

"Give me a ride?"

"Sure! Is Jacob home?"

"Of course! It's Sunday. Pot roast's on."

"I was hoping you'd say that."

I pulled Jacob out of mom's recliner and took them both for a spin. Jacob insisted on getting behind the wheel, so I hopped in the back. After a little, I asked, "Mom, you want to give it a try?"

"No, I'm content to let my boys chauffeur me around," she said from shotgun.

When we got back, I asked them to sit with me at the small dinette. I stretched out and looked at my mom. "How about if we do something different for Thanksgiving?"

Mom's brows creased. "What like a ham?"

I chuckled. "No, I was thinking of taking you both somewhere special. I want to celebrate my family."

Jacob's face split into a grin. "What did you have in mind, bro?"

"We used to talk about going to New York City, remember that?" I asked.

Jacob nodded. "Of course! The Big Apple's been a dream of mine."

"I went when I was a little girl," Mom said, her voice getting soft, "and saw the Rockettes with my parents. That was an incredible show."

"Well, let me make a few phone calls and see what I can arrange. I have a few ideas."

TWENTY-FOUR

The air around the table became charged with excitement, as they each contemplated the trip. It felt amazing to finally be *able* to afford to treat my mom the way she deserved. I couldn't wait to start making reservations for the holiday the following month.

After dinner, as was our tradition, Jacob and I strolled out to the front porch. The sun was setting early these days, so I put on a sweater and took a seat.

"Congratulations," Jacob said, toasting our drinks. "Owning your own clinic. That's incredible."

"Thanks!" I said warmly. "Right back at you! I know the work you put in to get your real estate license. Have you put in your notice yet?"

Jacob looked out onto the street and nodded slowly. "Last week. And Chuck Robertson's going to let me hang my license with him."

I whistled low. "Sweet! Well done. Robertson's got to be one of the best brokers in Chicago."

"Yeah, but turnover's high," he said quietly.

"Real estate isn't the easiest business, but I have faith in you."

"Any advice?"

I spent the next two hours coaching him on how to start up, giving him ideas on outreach and connecting with the right people. "You need to stand out. Model yourself after the other successful realtors, and go the extra mile!"

He nodded, soaking it all in. After that, I vowed to follow up with him on the phone twice a week. He made me proud by not only putting in the time to succeed, but by consistently asking for my help then applying what I was teaching him. He quickly started seeing results.

The following month we left for New York and I purchased a suite at the Plaza Hotel. This palatial landmark didn't disappoint with its Beaux-Arts décor. I wanted to treat my family to something above and beyond anything they'd ever experienced. The Plaza was the iconic hotel to show them just how much I adored them both.

I had researched the best restaurants New York had to offer and made reservations for each night. I also purchased excellent seats to the play Mom had been talking about for years, Wicked. We also enjoyed the simple pleasures of walking through Central Park and down the streets of Manhattan.

The last night we were enjoying Carbone's signature white lasagna when Mom pushed her plate forward a few inches and said, "I can't eat another bite."

"You liked it?"

"Yes," she said, giving me a meaningful look. "I've loved every moment of this long weekend. When I get home, I'm going to develop the film and frame at least a half dozen of the photos for my walls."

"I really need to get you a digital camera, Mom," I said with a grin. "No one develops film anymore."

She shook her head. "I'm fine with my relic. You've done enough for me. This was a trip filled with beautiful memories."

"It's my pleasure."

She reached out her hand and touched mine. "You've really made it, Billy. I'm so proud of you!"

My cheeks flushed. "Thanks, Mom!"

"Do you remember when you were thirteen, and I took you to see John Maxwell speak?"

"Of course," I said. "I remember that night well!" Mom had always made a point to put me in front of as many good role models as she could. John Maxwell was an author, speaker and pastor who spoke from his heart to inspire people to live their lives to the fullest. He struck a chord within me when he proclaimed that the world needed more leaders. His words encouraged me to remain focused and lead by example. "That evening, I realized that if I applied myself the next day would always be better than today."

"Well, you're living proof of his message!" she said, spreading her arms out to indicate the room around her. "Today is far better than yesterday was and if I'm not mistaken the day after will be even better! You're a shining example of how hope inspires change."

"Thank you, Mom," I murmured. "I really want to inspire others to find their inner greatness, too. I have been doing some public speaking and want to do more."

"You should do that!" Jacob cried. "You always inspire me."

Mom leaned forward. "You really should share your story with others. It's remarkable what you've done. People need to hear about it."

I thought about what Mom said all the way home and into the next week. Ever since I was young, I'd always felt called to impact the lives of people through public speaking. I wanted to help them create a better blueprint to living a fulfilled life. Over the prior year I'd managed to get in front of a few groups, giving keynotes, but I'd always had to pay to be there.

The following Thursday, I began speaking up more at our group meetings. In addition, I took Adam under my wing and began working with him. After I obtained ownership of my own clinic, he was inspired to stretch himself out of his comfort zones and expand his practice.

I'd find ways to get in front of people anyway I could, expanding to talk to other business communities as well. If given the opportunity, I'd pay to be a speaker at a company retreat. It was expensive, but that seemed the only way to share my knowledge with large groups. There was no greater feeling then seeing the hope on a person's face in the audience, like the one I had when Maxwell spoke many years before.

Everything was coming together. Only one key area of my life was missing, but I was well aware of it. Although I'd dated, I was still waiting to meet a woman I could connect with on a meaningful level. As if I didn't have enough frustration about still being single, my mom continually reminded me that she would like to have grandkids.

During a Cinco de Mayo celebration, Adam and I were sitting in the garden patio of a tequila lounge off Milwaukee Avenue. We were halfway through our first margarita, when his girlfriend Candace joined us. She gave Adam a look that made me smile. I wanted what they had.

Allowing them a moment of privacy, I looked around the small enclosed area and caught the eye of a tall, dark skinned beauty with long brown hair. Drawn to her movements across the room, I watched her approached a crowded table of revelers. She greeted her friends then turned to shoot me an infectious smile that left me wearing a silly grin.

As I continued to follow her movements, the rest of the world tuned out around me. This amazing woman cast out an alpha type confidence, which radiated all around her, as she interacted with her friends.

I have to meet her!

For a few moments, I was content to watch her laugh and chat with her friends. I knew I was staring, but didn't care. She was an absolute beauty. I glanced over at Candace and Adam, who were deep in conversation. Feeling brave, I slipped away from our table and approached the mysterious woman who'd stolen my heart with one glance.

Not sure what I was going to say, I made my way to her through the throngs of people. When I was a few feet away, she spun around, gave me a warm look and said, "We're heading to a little Italian place down the street. Wanna come?"

As if in a trance I nodded, before I realized I wasn't alone. "I'm with some friends," I said, feeling a burst of disappointment.

"Bring them," came her quick reply.

I thought about it for a moment. "I don't want to," I said with a slow grin.

She matched my smile. "Then don't."

I nodded, enjoying the simplicity of her statement. "Give me a few minutes," I said.

I walked back to our table and caught the amused smiles of Candace and Adam. They seemed to understand my intent without my saying a word.

"Go," Adam said. "Have fun."

I nodded. "Thanks!"

As I walked back to the woman, her friends were all getting up from their table, putting on their jackets.

"We got a cab. You coming?" she asked.

"Sure," I said, quickly deciding to leave my car behind. It was far more intimate to squeeze into a cab with her.

When the cab arrived and everyone began piling in, we realized there wasn't enough room. Not allowing the inconvenience to deter her, she turned to whisper, "Guess I'll have to sit on your lap."

I couldn't believe my good fortune. This potentially awkward situation made it very easy to get to know this beauty. Her name was Hannah and she was a Doctor of Psychology, doing post-doctorate work at a school for children on the autism spectrum. We talked all through dinner then stayed up past midnight sharing our lives one story after another. It was amazing how much we had in common.

Being that she was half Italian and half Hungarian, Hannah talked with her hands, which further enchanted me. As we continued to share thoughts, I realized her dreams for the future matched mine perfectly. And we weren't afraid to dream greatly.

We also agreed we wanted children, two or three. That night I think we discussed every subject possible and this woman came up perfect in every way. We made plans to get together the next day at my home after work. I sent an enormous bouquet of flowers to her school then attempted to cook an Italian dish my mom had taught me long ago. By the end of the second day, we were both madly in love.

The moment Hannah left, I called Mom. "I just met the woman I'm going to marry!"

TWENTY-FIVE

It didn't take long before Hannah and I were engaged. I continued to expand the business, more motivated than ever. I was pleased when our little Thursday night group grew to the point where we needed a hotel conference room to fit all the attendees. Entrepreneurs from a variety of businesses began showing up, looking for advice and mentorship. People happily chipped in a few bucks to cover the cost of the room and I took over leading the meetings.

Victor, a young entrepreneur who attended regularly, had branched off from his father's successful company and was eager to make it on his own. He was an inventor with a fresh patent for a robotic kitchen gadget that had the potential to take the world by storm. He reached out to me after a seminar I gave on word-of-mouth marketing.

"How are the online reviews coming along?" I asked him. I had taken a special interest in this nineteen-year-old genius and offered to give him more one-on-one coaching.

"Got another eight yesterday and fifty-two promising to review next week."

"Good, about a third should come through. How are sales?"

"They're coming along, double from last month," he said then paused for a moment. "The numbers are still low, though."

"Double is great!" I said. "What else are you doing to get your product out there?"

He shrugged. "I've been focused on online sales. I'm using a system that's a whole selling engine."

I nodded. "That's good, but you have to hit marketing from all angles. Have you written a press release?"

"No," he said. "I didn't think about that."

"Come on, let's grab a bite. I'll give you some ideas!"

I spent the next few weeks giving him lots of advice and concrete plans for expanding his online presence and tapping into his customer base. We boosted his social media, created an affiliate market base, built him a website and wrote a few press releases which were picked up by local papers. He was eager to learn and apply everything I could teach him.

Victor soaked up everything like a sponge, building from my ideas. I also gave him several books to read. Within a few months, he had more orders than he could handle, so I guided him to build a fulfillment center to handle the shipping.

I discovered that Victor's father, Mr. Dorian, owned a large chain of supermarkets in the area. He was so happy with his son's success that he invited me to dine at Fogo de Chao Brazilian Steakhouse one day to express his gratitude. I enjoyed sharing the step by step plans I'd laid out for Victor. Mr. Dorian listened with rapt attention and even asked me for advice on social media for his business.

About a week later, a man dressed in a three-piece suit walked into my clinic. I happened to be at the front desk when he approached. I gave him a smile, thinking he must be a referral from one of my patients.

"How can I help you?" I asked.

"Sir, Mr. Dorian sent me to ask if you might like to be our keynote speaker at our next convention in Vegas."

Wow, that would be a nice step up!

"Sure, that sound great," I said. "And how much would that run?" Normally, the fee was a few hundred to speak at a convention, but since Dorian had hundreds of markets around the country, I could only imagine it would cost a pretty penny.

He gave me a puzzled look. "Well, sir," he said slowly. "I think that Mr. Dorian would like to pay you your normal fee."

"Oh," I stammered, feeling my face flush red. *He wants to pay me. That's new!* I cleared my throat then said, "Can I get back to you on that?"

"Sure," he said.

I waited a full thirty seconds after he left before I let out a loud cry of delight. "Brene, do you know what this means?"

She nodded excitedly. She knew about my goals and deep desire to branch into leadership speaking. "Your dream is happening!"

"Yes, it is!"

Two years passed and things just continued to improve. Overwhelmed with emotion, I looked down at my newborn daughter in my arms. The admiration I felt for my wife, as well as all woman who go through childbirth, soared to new heights. It was my privilege to hold Hannah's hand throughout the process and I felt humbled to cradle the precious product of that labor.

As Bianca's eyes flittered closed, a sense of overwhelming thankfulness and love encompassed me. My mom's face flickered into my mind. The challenges that came from living on a tight budget and going without must have been so much for her to handle. All the night classes she took to earn her master's degree, while working three jobs to support me and Jacob, was hard to imagine. Her love for us was never-ending, but the financial pressures on her strong shoulders must have so much to bear.

Fortunately, I continued to reach new levels of success with my clinic. Despite its tiny space, we continued to expand past the thin walls, as if it magically could hold quadruple its normal capacity. The testimonials coming from the patients inspired me and my team.

In addition, I had dozens of coaching clients, coming from various businesses and walks of life. Jacob had just won his second quarterly award at his real estate office. Working with a mortgage broker, he even helped Mom purchase our childhood home the previous summer. After a lot of coaxing, she had finally accepted my help and allowed me to give her the required down payment.

With Brene's help, I was booked out for weekend seminars for the next few months. Thanks to numerous newspaper and magazine articles, I was filling auditoriums with people interested in hearing me inspire their leader within.

Life was everything I could have ever wanted, and more.

TRUST

Dear Bianca,

It was such a blessing to be present during your birth, little lady. One of the things that drew me to your mom was her inner power and confidence. However, let me tell you I had no idea how tremendous her strength truly was until I witnessed her champion fifteen hours of labor.

I'll admit, I was ready to cry uncle, but your mom never gave up, never discarded her birth plan. All I could do was hold her hand, give her cold compresses, rub her back and watch the miracle of you unfold.

In your first year, she was your shadow. She did everything for you and never complained of clear sleep deprivation. I picked up every book about fatherhood that I could, but soon realized how silly that was. Needless to say, I bowed to her as our family leader that year.

I pray that you will surround yourself with people that will pick you up when you are down, who will support you in hard times, *because there will be tough moments, Sweetheart. If you pick the right people, the right tribe, they will stand by you and fight alongside you, no matter the battles.*

And remember, I will always be your biggest fan.

Love,

Dad

TWENTY-SIX

Hannah and I were sitting on the floor with Bianca, laughing at her antics as she pulled herself up into a standing position. She bounced up and down in delight, squealing with happiness at our applause. It was a rare lazy Sunday morning, one where neither Hannah or I had anything to do.

When the phone rang, I grimaced slightly at the interruption. Glancing at the cell's screen, I relaxed. It wasn't work. It was Jacob.

"Hey, bro," I said. "How's the open house?" He had scored Mrs. Brehman's palatial estate in Lincoln Park last week.

"Bill..." I could hear his voice catch in his throat. My heart hammered in my chest as I stood up and walked off a few steps.

"What's wrong?" Hannah whispered after me.

I held up a finger to let her know I'd fill her in as soon as I could. "Jacob? You OK?"

"It's Mom," he began, then burst into tears.

"What? You're scaring me. Is she OK?"

"No, she passed away last night."

"What?" I shouted. I felt my body slam against the dining room wall. Slipping to the floor, I gripped the phone to my ear as if it were a life line.

"She didn't tell us. She had cancer," he said, his voice broken with sobs. "The doctor just told me. She'd been struggling for months. The cancer metastasized to her brain. Her bone. Her organs —all over."

"How is that possible?" I asked. I didn't hear the answer, because the phone suddenly became too heavy to hold. I felt it slip from my hands and clunk to the ground, as Hannah came to my rescue. She quickly ended the call with Jacob and held me.

Unable to cope with the loss, I spiraled into all-consuming grieving despair. I drank bourbon day and night until I fell into a stupor. I wanted so desperately to avoid the pain. Mom was everything to me, she carried me through most of my life, giving every single part of herself. How could she not tell me she had cancer? How could I go on without her?

Whenever the booze wore off enough for me to be lucid, snapshots of memories would spin around me, like a collage. Blowing seven candles from a two-layer chocolate cake she'd made, riding a pony at a fair, throwing breadcrumbs at a pair of Mallards at the park, sharing a soda at a fast food restaurant, being tucked into bed, all blended together with a complete disregard for time. Wanting to dull the ache in my heart and head, I'd reach for the next bottle to quiet the voices of recollection.

I was in a fog for the following few days. Hannah and Jacob guided me through the memorial and I robotically acknowledged everyone who came to share their sympathy. I did what was required, plastering a small smile on my face. They knew it was fake, but It didn't matter. Didn't I deserve sympathy from everyone around me? They'd understand and if they didn't, I couldn't care less.

Hannah took care of me, tenderly making sure I ate enough. I couldn't keep down much, so she'd make chicken broth soup with vegetables. I stopped acknowledging her presence and shut myself away from the world in our guestroom.

One morning, I woke up less dizzy to the sound of laughter. It was my daughter in the other room. Suddenly, I recognized the existence of another long enough to tear myself away from my self-pity.

I propped myself up by the door frame, watching Hannah help Bianca with her daily exercises. It was something she and I had always done together. As I continued to be a spectator, something rumbled in the back of my mind. A remembrance of an old familiar emotion, something other than the self-loathing and hatred, emotions I'd worn like a comfortable blanket for the last few days.

Love.

I loved these two with all of my heart. Watching them, my love for them slowly extinguished the angry emotions that had overtaken me. Then, as the combined effect of the bourbon from the last few days coursed through my system in one flush, I became violently ill. I raced to the bathroom and allowed my body to relieve itself of everything it could. I heaved and retched until it finally subsided.

When I had the strength, I pulled myself up and studied my reflection. An intense jolt ran through me. Gone was the vibrant, healthy man, I considered myself to be. In its place was a haggard reflection of a man that more resembled my bitter father than anyone I knew. Disgusted, I heaved again and again.

Finally spent, I crumpled to the ground and shook my head. How had I allowed this to happen? Mom certainly wouldn't have sanctioned it, if she were alive. What an ultimate betrayal to her memory to indulge in this selfishness. Pulling myself up, I showered and stumbled out to the living room, where Hannah seemed to register my lucid gaze. Silently, she embraced me with all the love I knew she felt the day we exchanged vows.

"I'm so sorry," I cried. "I can't believe I've been such a—"

She put two fingers up to my lips and shook her head. "There's no need, sweetheart."

It took me a couple days to be able to walk through the front doors of my clinic. That day I called Brene who was relieved to hear from me. She let me know that everyone in the clinic understood. My team had simply told my patients and coaching clients that I needed a few days.

I was humbled to discover that my business ran like a well-oiled machine in my absence. Dr. Tim's associate doctor had stepped in to treat my clients. In addition, Lewis, who was now in his final year at my alma mater and precepting at our clinic, also assisted with the patient load.

When I walked in the door of the clinic, Brene jumped up and catapulted herself into my arms. I tried to apologize to her and the rest of the team, but no one would allow me to get out the words. It was clear that they were my tribe, my team, my family and nothing I could do would ever sway them from my side.

RESPONSIBILITY

Dear Bianca,

Months after you were born, I wrote this poem to myself.

I will admit the responsibility of being a father terrifies me because I am far from perfect. I wanted to keep being an example for you in the forefront of my mind, and remind myself to always take ownership of my life.

I love you so much!

I AM...

I am the one responsible for my rise. I am the one responsible for my fall. I am responsible for the sun shining on my face in the morning. I am responsible for the rain pouring on my head in the evening. I am responsible for my experiences, my circumstances and all events to this point. I take full responsibility for each decision that I have ever made, and will make. I take full responsibility for my actions that reveal my character. I am fully in charge of my attitude, and thus my happiness. I claim responsibility for my ambitions and desires for my own life. I admit responsibility for my focus and attention. The love I receive is based on my responsibility to give love to those around me and to myself. It is because of my admittance to this, the responsibility for my complete self, that I am free. I am free to grow, develop and flourish, for the world is now open to me.

I do not make excuses for that which I am responsible. I do not complain, for I will either change my circumstance or remove myself from it. I do not procrastinate; I initiate and persevere towards the desires of my soul. I do not empower my problems, I ask myself how I created them and work diligently to resolve. I am in control of myself and my emotions. I know that bad things do not happen to me, they just happen, as they do to all people. I refuse to blame anyone, for blame cripples my mind and weakens my spirit.

I will be responsible for all areas of my life. Responsibility will actualize my highest potential. I know that a fulfilled life is not entitled, and no one is in command of my life but me. I realize that I illuminate to others, and my actions will have a lasting effect. I will exercise my will every day of my life. I will take control and responsibility to live my life, never based on fear, but on my highest values.

Love,
Dad

ABOUT DR. BEN DUKE

Dr. Ben Duke is a nationally recognized speaker, author and mentor focused on Self-Leadership, as well as a Licensed Chiropractic Physician. With over 15 years spent studying the power of the mind and strategies grounded in psychology and neuroscience, Ben is the revolutionary developer of "The Leadership Hack" and creator of the "Adjusting for Leadership" Masterclass.

DrBenDuke.com

facebook.com/drbenduke

instagram.com/drbenduke

youtube.com/drbenduke

Made in the USA
Lexington, KY
14 June 2018